Something Understood
ART THERAPY IN CANCER CARE

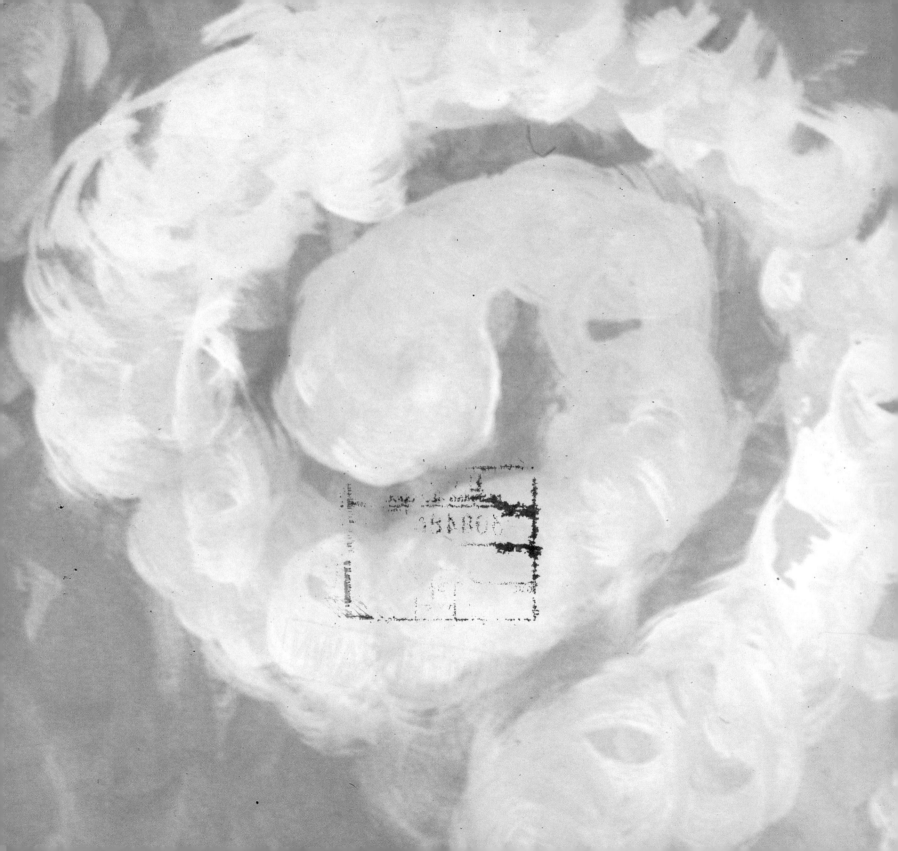

Something Understood
ART THERAPY IN CANCER CARE

Camilla Connell

WREXHAM PUBLICATIONS
in association with Azimuth Editions

This book is dedicated to all those who created its content – patients past and present at the Royal Marsden NHS Trust, London

First published in 1998 by
Wrexham Publications
Ealing Green
London W5 5EN

in association with
Azimuth Editions
1 Rowley Industrial Park
Roslin Road
London W3 8BH

The author and publishers would like to thank all those whose art work is reproduced in this book. Although a decision was made to protect all patients by anonymity, every effort has been made to contact the copyright holders for their permission. Any omissions are inadvertent and we will be happy to make corrections in a subsequent edition.

British Library Cataloguing-in-Publication Data
A catalogue record for this book is available from the British Library

ISBN 0 9533529 0 0

Edited by Jane Havell
Designed by Richard Foenander
Printed in Great Britain by PJ Reproductions Ltd

Contents

Acknowledgements

As an art therapy student in 1985 I had a close friend with cancer. The situation gave rise to some simple questions. Does someone with a life-threatening illness undergo experiences that are difficult or impossible to communicate to others? Do certain constraints on the patient – the desire to protect family and friends, and to preserve good relationships with carers – limit the degree to which he or she can voice their concerns? Indeed, are some feelings beyond words? I asked myself whether there might be a place for the use of art materials in a supportive, safe and impartial therapeutic environment – perhaps art therapy could enable the patient to find a more creative response to a difficult situation, and feel less of a victim.

At this time, art therapy in the context of an NHS oncology unit was unknown. I qualified, and began by observing the work of an art tutor who regularly held classes in the physiotherapy department of the Royal Marsden Hospital. I became accepted as an official volunteer, and was encouraged to visit patients in the palliative care unit who were too ill to attend the classes. The nurses always welcomed me, but one consultant remarked that he did not think I would find much to do with patients who were so seriously ill. After a year of quiet, anonymous work, I was invited by the charge nurse on the ward to give a short paper and talk to the other nurses, to help them understand better what I was trying to do. My paper came to the notice of the manager of the new rehabilitation unit, and when it opened in the spring of 1989 I was invited to join it part-time as an official member of staff.

After ten years of rewarding therapeutic work, I have written this book with two purposes in mind. It is an attempt to distill and pass on to others some of the many learning experiences I have had, and also to make known to a wider number of people the immense potential of art therapy, both for those living with cancer and for therapists dealing in related work within oncology.

I stand indebted between two groups of people – those who have provided the unique material for the book, patients past and present at the Royal Marsden Hospital, and those who have contributed so readily and enthusiastically towards putting the project together.

The latter group includes Millie Potucek, Paul Hyett and Steve Millward of the Photographic Department at the hospital. Without their continual support and excellent work in creating a permanent record of art made over many years, this volume would never have seen the light of day.

Jane Havell and Richard Foenander, the editor and designer of the book, stood by me for the whole time, encouraging me to keep going with the fundraising and never doubting the value of publishing the work. Their talents and enthusiasm, and their understanding of the need for quality in offering these pictorial testimonies to a wider public, have resulted in this beautifully designed volume.

The Omega Foundation, The Corinne Burton Memorial Trust and Zeneca Pharmaceuticals gave valuable support in helping to fund the project (more details about them can be found on page 147).

The Fund Raising Department of the Royal Marsden Hospital, Marie Curie Cancer Care, Macmillan Cancer Relief, Breast Cancer Care, The Hospice Information Service, The British Association of Art Therapists and The Diocese of London helped by promoting the book through their mailing lists.

Michael Baum, Joan Woddis and Ian Kerr brought a very necessary wider view to the text, providing a supportive and rigorous framework to enable me to write it in the only way I could.

I am grateful in every respect to James, who has kept me on the straight but not so narrow for most of a lifetime.

To one and all, many thanks.

Camilla Connell
London 1998

Preface

Professor Michael Baum, ChM, FRCS
Institute of Surgical Studies, University College Hospital Medical School

Some time in 1990, shortly after I was appointed Professor of Surgery at the Royal Marsden Hospital, I was making a solitary ward round, checking on the welfare of my breast cancer patients, when I came upon an unfamiliar woman handing out pots of paint to a patient recovering from my surgical assault. Assuming she was an occupational therapist and wanting to make my presence felt, I engaged her in conversation. Within five minutes of talking to Camilla Connell, I was totally won over to the concept of art therapy for patients with cancer. Since that day, a warm relationship has developed between us, based on mutual respect and understanding for the contributions we can each make to patients recovering from cancer surgery or, for that matter, any other life-threatening disorder.

My interest and enthusiasm can be described at two levels. First, there is an uncanny thematic similarity running through the works of many of these patients who face serious disease. It is as if the experience of cancer stimulates some deeply hidden communal memory to evoke the symbolism of life and death, fear and hope. The tree, for example, is a recurring theme in these works of art, one that can be traced back through many cultures to the original *etz chaim* (tree of life) of the Old Testament.

At an individual level, what I have found so moving is the obvious cathartic value of using art to express hidden fears; the progression of the imagery from fear to hope as a sign of recovery and, sadly, in the reverse direction, as a sign of deterioration. There is no doubt that art is a powerful medium for self-expression for frightened patients who do not have the words or the will to express themselves verbally.

Many patients have hidden talents, yet even in the absence of conventional artistic skill some of the almost childlike and naive pictures are enormously expressive and deeply moving to the observer. I believe that art therapy is a unique vehicle for allowing patients with cancer to express hidden emotions and thus, to some extent, provide their own psychotherapy.

As a practical expression of my enthusiasm and support, I helped Camilla organise an exhibition of the patients' art, which was shown first at the Royal Marsden Hospital and then continued as a peripatetic exhibition around medical centres in the UK. I also used my authority to help raise funding for a second part-time art therapist to work at the Sutton branch of our institution.

While this was going on, the Marsden, like other cancer centres in London, was facing closure as a result of the Tomlinson Report on the future of London hospital services. As Professor of Surgery and Director of Clinical Research, I was placed in the front line of the battle to save the hospital. This was also at a time when planning blight led to the early retirement of one of my consultant colleagues and the departure of another for a different teaching hospital. I was left to run the department virtually single-handed.

The stress of this workload and our uncertain future were almost too much to bear. I placed myself at Camilla's mercy to provide art therapy for my own struggle. I elected to undertake private tuition in portrait sculpture (which is her particular expertise). I learnt at first hand the benefits of self-expression through the medium of clay. The journey through a lifeless lump of material to a recognisable portrait of my daughter was sufficiently cathartic to help me cope with my struggles (I suspect that some of my fiercest attacks on the clay were surrogates for physical abuse of the bureaucrats who were trying to destroy the wonderful institution of the Royal Marsden Hospital).

I therefore have both first- and secondhand experience of the power of art therapy. I acknowledge that this is anecdotal evidence and, as a clinical scientist, I would not accept art therapy on these merits alone – but I truly believe that it has a part to play in the management of the sick and the frightened, and that it is also a topic suitable for scientific evaluation using established instruments for the monitoring of patients' quality of life.

Good medicine is not only the practice of the science of the subject, but also the practice of the humanities of the subject. Central to the humanitarian practice of medicine is the development of good communication skills. Central to the development of good communication skills is the development of empathy. Strictly, empathy means trying to get inside the patient's head, to feel his or her fears and pain, a task that even the most empathetic of doctors can find extremely difficult. As far as I am concernd, art therapy is the most direct line into the patient's experience of illness, and I feel almost ashamed that I do not make use of it in the day-to-day practice of my own clinic. Perhaps there simply are not enough Camilla Connells to go round. If there were, I have little doubt that the drugs budget for the NHS would fall, as prescriptions for anxyolitics and anti-depressants would be replaced by the prescription of art therapy.

Foreword

The title of this book provides a context for everything that follows. These two words, 'something understood', embody what could be the one aspiration informing the discipline of art therapy in cancer care. After addressing the diverse situations that will be described in these pages, what more could be hoped for, in the face of the mystery of our existence, that something should be understood? Not everything, by any means, and maybe not much, but 'something' that may help a person through the course of illness whatever the outcome. These two words, taken from the close of George Herbert's poem 'Prayer' (see page 126), give us a sense of a scale of possibilities from zero to infinity.

Before the written word was part of our heritage, art was used to communicate spiritual and psychological truths. Imagery has always been central to the dissemination of traditional knowledge. When we regard works of art – such as those of the Egyptians, or the early Italian period – we feel that something was understood by its makers. It is hard to express these feelings in words, but the life in these art works is still being transmitted to us even in our time. Are we perhaps losing this capacity, in spite of the enormous leaps in our civilisation? The healing, reintegrating effects of art are seldom felt or sought for in contemporary modes of image-making. None the less, the creative instinct is present in us all, although it can take many different forms. The impulse to make art springs from our need to communicate and validate our inner world in a way that will not betray or destroy the material that is found there: Jung suggests that 'the happy state is the creative state'.[1]

Although we value our works of art, the process itself of making art is undervalued in present-day education and has been for decades. It seems that when children reach a certain age academic achievement becomes all-important and creative opportunities are reduced. This undervaluing of the creative process is maintained in further education and adult life, where pressures to achieve and survive in a technological and materialistic world cause us to measure success in terms of statistics and verifiable outcomes. However, only the phenomenal world can be subject to these processes; the noumenal – the no less real but unseen world, unavailable to the outer senses – defies such methods of validation. Here lies one root of the problem. A certain amount of lip service is now paid to the idea of a holistic approach to illness. However, in a fairly new discipline such as art therapy the perceived, somewhat mysterious, nature of its action leaves its inquisitors in the medical profession with a sense of bewilderment and hence suspicion when it comes to incorporating it within a strictly scientific treatment regime.

It was said by the eminent psychiatrist Maurice Nicoll that medicine is an art not a science. In the relatively new speciality of palliative care, doctors seem to have a predisposition towards understanding a statement of this kind. Alongside all their finely tuned scientific skills, a greater awareness exists of the psychological and spiritual needs of their patients. In some of the hospices in the UK, an emphasis is indeed placed on this element.

In the absence of research (notoriously difficult to achieve in art therapy), we look to the evidence presented by the people who are living with cancer – it is they who, once their interest was evoked and their anxieties allayed, have provided the material which constitutes this book. It will show how for some people in an NHS cancer hospital a new exploration can begin, the goal of which may be unknown yet deeply wished for. Art making may feel like a form of play, yet it can be life-enhancing – even if it is just the copying of a get-well card. It offers a unique potential for allowing, exploring, experimenting, discovering and enlightening.

1 *W*ays of working

What happens in art therapy? Many people ask this question and it can only be answered in part. What happens is always different, always unique to the individual and often quite inspiring (even mysterious), but it is hardly ever without some change for the better in the psychological state of the patient. For one thing, it requires him or her to be active – itself a valuable element in a hospital environment where passivity is encouraged and sometimes indeed desirable.

Patients in a cancer hospital are there for the treatment of a physical illness; they are not, in principle, looking for a psychological therapy, and their responses can range from enthusiasm and curiosity through to indifference, even anxiety. Art therapy is still largely unknown and unfamiliar. It does not fall into the expected categories of tests and physical treatments. But it can help a person to find a contact with their inner world more quickly and deeply than many other means, and I have come to the conclusion that this function could be its most important aim.

In the hospital where I work, the art therapy service is available to all patients, whatever their status. Some people begin while they are in the hospital and others have found it more useful to come as outpatients, perhaps combining a session in art therapy with another appointment such as radiotherapy. The therapy can be offered in three ways – first, on an individual basis with the therapist, secondly in a group, and thirdly by working while in the ward at times of one's own choosing and without the constant presence of the therapist. Each offers different possibilities.

Individual sessions

These take place in the art therapy room and last for one hour, with the therapist present throughout. The patient may choose which materials to use, how to use them and how to apportion the time between art work and talking if he wishes. Reading or writing may also be involved as the situation is very flexible. The therapist does not maintain a silent inscrutability, but endeavours to encourage and support the patient where needed, especially in getting started and in the use of materials. The value of one-to-one sessions lies in the possibility of dialogue between patient, image and therapist, and the opportunity to find release from the pressure of feelings in a confidential setting away from the surroundings in which the patient usually finds himself.

Group sessions

These share aspects with individual treatment, but have the additional benefit of sharing work and of talking with others. Much can be given and received by members of a group in an atmosphere of mutual understanding. For some patients this is the preferred choice from the beginning, while others often feel ready to come after one or two individual sessions.

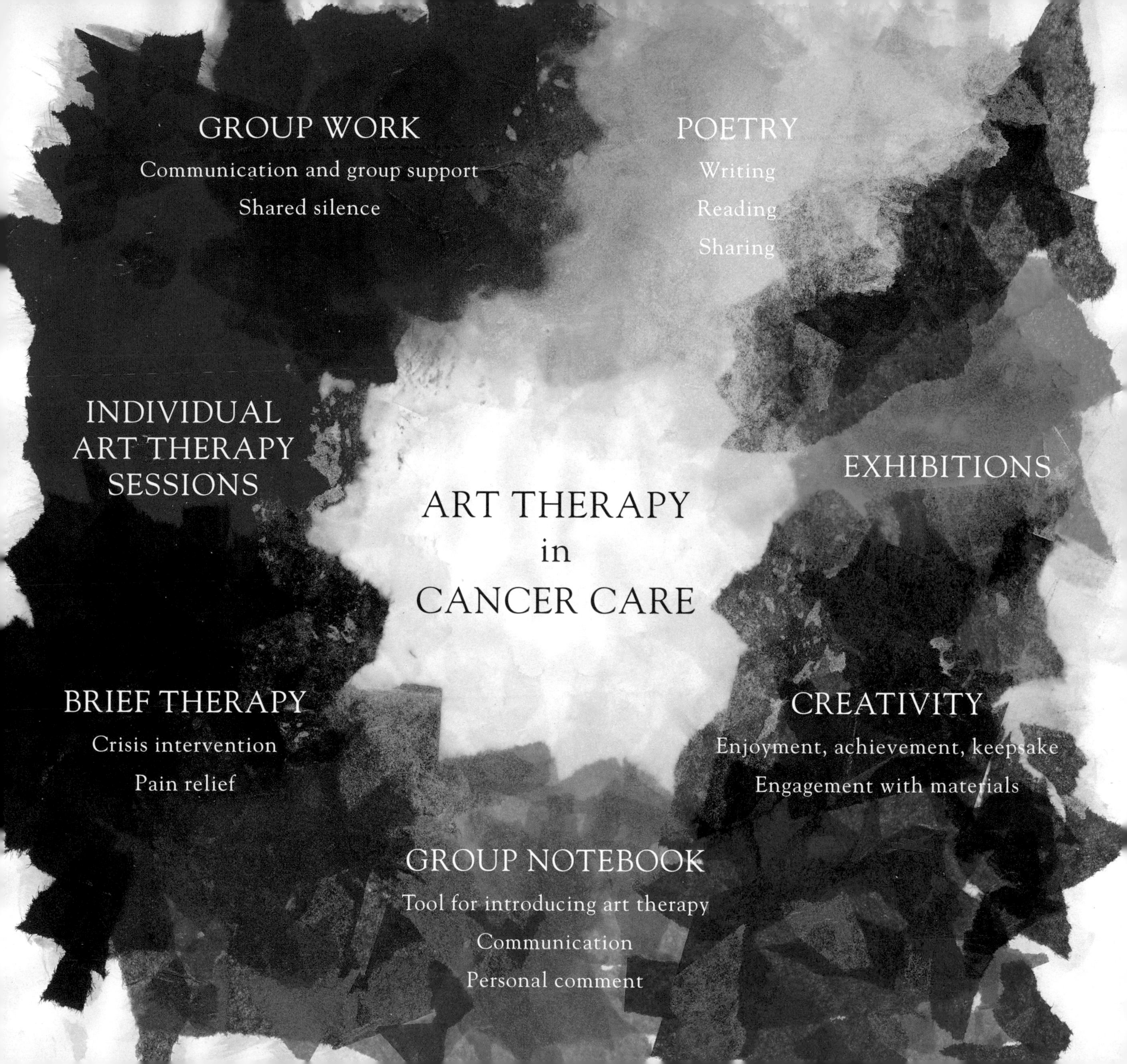

GROUP WORK
Communication and group support

Shared silence

POETRY
Writing

Reading

Sharing

INDIVIDUAL
ART THERAPY
SESSIONS

EXHIBITIONS

ART THERAPY
in
CANCER CARE

BRIEF THERAPY

Crisis intervention

Pain relief

CREATIVITY

Enjoyment, achievement, keepsake

Engagement with materials

GROUP NOTEBOOK

Tool for introducing art therapy

Communication

Personal comment

I have been running group sessions for many years now, and every week there are new faces as well as familiar ones. With patients living under a range of constraints – of illness, treatment schedules and travel arrangements – it is an open and flexible event. A group of between three and nine people assemble once a week for two hours in the afternoon. After brief introductions and, for the benefit of newcomers, an outline of the group's purpose and the way it will proceed, materials are introduced: water-based paint, pastels, crayons, felt-tip pens, inks, oil-paint sticks, collage materials, clay and a variety of paper.

Then comes the question, how to start? This is a challenging moment. A pristine sheet of paper lies on the drawing board, materials that often have not been encountered since schooldays stand beside the paper. What to do? Responses are varied, but even for those familiar with paints and crayons there is still a moment of questioning. There are other feelings, too – fear, for example, of appearing a fool because one is not expert, wonder at how to handle the materials, and concern at an apparent absence of ideas. But there can also be excitement and anticipation. Here, away from their normal hospital role of being passive, patients must reorientate themselves to be active as in ordinary life, because they have agreed to try something different. They have come to the art therapy room on the understanding that they will be engaging in a process which can be largely unknown and also personal – moreover, in the company of strangers.

A certain anxiety can be detected in remarks such as, 'What am I meant to do?', 'I haven't got any imagination,' 'I can't even draw a straight line,' 'All the other people here are so good.' The response to the last is usually, 'Don't worry, we were like you when we started.' This initial moment of difficulty is soon over. There are many ways to begin. Some people are excited by the colours, others have such a need for release from inner feelings that they will launch in with the biggest brush and the thickest paint to channel their energy. To the patients' surprise, sometimes it is the very physical motions employed that trigger their feelings.

For others it can be different: if they need more help it is important that it is not withheld. Art therapy is not some frightening trial of ability or capacity for expression. Sometimes words can help, such as 'experiment', 'explore', and sometimes suggestions such as 'only colours and shapes', 'cover the paper as fast as you can, no thinking' or 'just choose the colour that attracts you most'. Reading poetry or talking around a theme can help call on the image-making capacity of the brain, a constructive use of imagination. Finally, if the first step seems impossible, the therapist can join the patient on the same sheet of paper, each with brush or crayon in hand; they can make marks for each other in a sort of dialogue until the patient is free enough to

One patient arrived early for her session to tell me the pessimistic news she had just received about the progress of her illness. She said she was completely blank. We considered poetry and literature, but discarded that approach. We sat close together, and I said I would make a mark for her on the paper and maybe she could respond with one for me. I hoped in this way to start her off and that she could then develop the image for herself.

I began with a small yellow mark and she went on with black, making a hill shape. I partly filled in the profile. She then made a black zig-zag right across the paper, stating with some satisfaction that it was the first time since her bad news that she had been able to express her anger. Mild anxiety arose in me as I drew a thin yellow line through the tops of the zig-zag. As we worked into the shapes, I felt anger in myself for her situation and used the crayon very hard across the bottom of the paper, making a loud squeaking noise.

She liked this noise and replied with a magenta zig-zag up the side of the page equally noisily – the screech, she said, was an expression of her inner pain. She added that if an elderly woman had not also been in the room she would have screamed out loud.

I tried to stay with what was happening on the paper and respond to that. I also had an impulse to try to ground her, to keep her down on earth to prevent flights of anxious fantasy. A pink spiral on one shape made her see a fish's head coming up out of the water. She then began to soften the hard lines of the chalk with her fingers, enjoying how it felt and saying it was like talcum powder. As she did this, the angry feelings seemed to soften. Afterwards she spoke of how she valued the *process*. I began to realise how my preconceptions and concerns had kept trying to take me away from a direct response to the image on the paper. There are many ways to explore this process of initiating and following someone's work.

proceed alone. For the therapist, creativity lies in finding ways to facilitate a beginning that is not too stressful. Once the process has started to flow it takes the direction most needed, provided there is not too much residual concern regarding the outcome, such as fear for self-respect and of the group as critics. Nobody likes to be seen as a fool.

As everyone settles down, silence ensues. Nothing

is imposed, but attention is gathered and focused in the work as there is often much to be committed to paper. As the silence deepens, one feels the concentration increase among people who arrived with fears, depression, preoccupations, tensions, pain, maybe nausea and headaches. The satisfaction to be derived from using art materials becomes evident – not only in the dab dab dab of colour upon colour, in the mixing of different hues, the sweep of a big brush or the detailed touch of a fine one, in dry paint, thick paint, watery paint, waxy crayons, soft charcoal crayons, the tearing of coloured tissue paper, but also in smearing, rubbing, scratching . . . There is a sensual delight in all these

CONFUSION.

Thoughts.
   Jungle of Thoughts
Want
~~Habitual~~ to see it
     in
Harmony, peace
     And
Order.

Oftnen Find it hard
        to
Manage it That Way.
     So
Generally it is a
Jungle fierce and disordered

processes, especially for someone rendered inactive, frustrated and seemingly ineffectual due to illness. Over and over again, the materials lend themselves to angry slashing and stabbing, to detailed painstaking work, to tender loving touches, to gaiety and carefree abandon, to gloom and despair, and through it all the appearance of a new and astonishing energy in even the most debilitated people.

An hour or more later they have to be reminded that time is nearly up. One by one they emerge from their work, some with surprise and remarks such as, 'The time has gone so fast,' and 'What has happened to my headache? It's disappeared.' A woman who had suffered disturbing tinnitus ever since undergoing brain surgery said, 'My tinnitus – it's not there for the first time since my operation, it's gone!' Others are visibly more relaxed, interested and animated, and allow their work to be displayed on the wall.

A break for refreshment is a good idea at this point. Not all therapists agree, but in the setting of a cancer hospital I think that gestures of normality and comfort are important. It also serves as a break between the 'doing' and the 'reflecting upon' the art work. A group of people, some of whom had arrived as strangers, are now as relaxed as if they had known each other for years, having shared this strangely intense, silent but very alive period of time. Now we turn our attention again to the pictures: arrayed on the wall they are somewhat distanced from their makers. Silently, for a moment, we contemplate the work, each his own but also other people's. This moment is important and should not be curtailed. In a life where social interaction usually means talking, to be able to communicate through silent empathy is a rare experience.

Eventually, someone will not be able to contain his observations or questions any longer and will begin to speak about his own work and ponder aloud on that of others. Some people are faintly bemused – a landscape is a landscape, and they may wish to find a focus only on the artistic qualities of a work. For some, the experience has been on a level as yet too profound for words. Those who do speak are listened to carefully, and each makes room for others to speak, telling of what their paintings mean for them and as much of their personal circumstances as they wish. Here, an occasional intervention by the therapist can be necessary so that all have a space to contribute, but otherwise the group will sustain itself, divulging and sharing hopes and fears, offering understanding born of experiences which many have in common.

Those in deep distress are not silenced by futile niceties, but listened to with the utmost respect. During this time, the pictures somehow act as vehicles for each person's inner situation. Time seems to melt away and when all have had their say, laughter, tears, compassion

all included, collectively we conclude the session. Each person recognises that such a degree of intimacy and intensity has its limitations – life cannot be lived in this atmosphere for too long. However, the mutual, shared support, which is so powerful, is an important aspect of a group such as this.

What of the art work, what happens to it? This is an interesting question. Whatever their feelings of artistic inadequacy, very few people destroy their efforts, at least not in the presence of the therapist. Sometimes the work can acquire the attributes of an icon, and come to hold a deep significance for their makers. Frequently, it accompanies patients back to the ward or

home, to be shown to others or kept as evidence of their plunge into the unknown on that particular afternoon. Others appear to find their achievement of little significance and will leave the room seemingly indifferent to the future of their work. If overwhelming feelings have been discharged in the painting, some patients definitely prefer to leave the work with the therapist. In this way they walk away freer from the burden with which they entered the room. Patients who attend regularly may name, date and store their work in individual folders made for them but left with the therapist for safe keeping. Later the pictures will be taken out and reviewed; they may become part of the patient's raison d'être and constitute something that affirms the life of that individual.

Working in the ward

The third and equally important routine that I undertake is to load a trolley with art materials and walk around the wards. It is here that many people first become aware of art therapy, although they may not wish or have much opportunity to pursue it at this stage. Patients in hospital are often kept busy. Admissions can be brief and treatment concentrated, with numbers of multidisciplinary staff needing to spend time with the patient. The patient may simply feel ill or be recovering from surgery.

However, some people may feel under-occupied or

over-anxious; they may dislike television and find they cannot concentrate on books, and welcome a chat and the possibility of borrowing something from the art trolley for the duration of their stay. I always have a number of drawing pads, good charcoal crayons, felt-tips pens, paints and drawing boards. The patient may not begin immediately, but the materials are there to pick up whenever they are wanted, maybe when a certain degree of privacy is possible, perhaps during the night if sleep proves difficult. The important thing is that the choice belongs entirely to the patient. Much can happen in these quiet interludes, and if the therapist is able to revisit the patient the work can be acknowledged and can form the basis for the three-cornered dialogue described earlier.

The group notebook

A useful tool that I have developed is a 'group notebook'. It is entitled 'Memories, Dreams, Reflections', the title of Jung's autobiography which seems best to describe what I envisage is the nature of its contents. It now occupies five volumes and continues to grow. It is an A4, two-ring, loose-leaf binder, with the art work inserted into clear plastic envelopes, back to back; this enhances the appearance of the work and enables it to be handled frequently without damage. It contains not only images, but poetry, prose and quotations.

This book serves several purposes. First, it offers some of the benefits of a cancer support group for those patients who cannot meet and are in the hospital on different units and at different times. Secondly, as a means of introducing myself and the idea of art therapy to people who are not familiar with it, it is a very helpful focus for an opening conversation. Thirdly, it reassures those who are anxious about their lack of skill, since it shows that most contributors are not very skilled in the formalities of art. Finally, if patients are encouraged by what they have looked at and wish to contribute something to the book themselves, they can see what media are available and make a choice about which they prefer to use.

2 Why?

Why indeed! Faced with an advanced and spreading breast cancer, a professional woman in her early fifties made this image while attending a group art therapy session in hospital. After fifteen years in remission, she could not believe that her illness had returned with such devastating effects on her life. As she drew the image in felt-tip pens, she remarked, 'everything is the wrong way round' – the fish, which reminded her of her Catholic background (the fish was the symbol for Christ used by the early Christians), are in the sky and the clouds are in the sea. Of the word 'WHY?' written in a large yellow flower-shape arising in the centre of the picture, she remarked, 'I was going to put "why me?" at first, but decided to leave it at just "why?".' Then followed heartfelt questions: why did she have no energy? Why did she have to be an invalid (she hated it so)? Why had the cancer come back after fifteen years just as the doctor had told she was clear? Why, when she had a lovely Georgian house and wanted to give dinner parties in it, could she do nothing? Her questions were many and painful.

In spite of her utter incomprehension of her situation, I was very struck by her feeling that the yellow flower should bear the word 'why?' and not 'why me?' In deciding this, she had raised her question to another level – that of a real enquiry, rather than a perception of her illness purely as an unjust personal affliction. This little word can be uttered in so many ways. It is with us before we begin to reason, because this impulse to question is our birthright and fundamental to our human nature. As life proceeds, the question mark is often extinguished by an insistence on answers; however, since our lives are lived on many levels the question still lies within and its resonance is particularly felt in times of great difficulty. It is a fundamental question that needs no answer – as we see in this picture, it opens like a flower!

I am very struck by the similarities between this pictorial image and the verbal images obtaining in the ancient religion of the Golden Elixir of Life (Chin Tan Chiao) that originated in eighth-century China. In *The Secret of the Golden Flower* we are told of 'the work towards an inner rebirth by means of contact with the circulation of the Light, and the creation of the divine kernel.' One short passage from this remarkable text states: 'The seed-blossom of the human body must be concentrated upward in the empty space. Immortality is contained in this sentence and also the overcoming of the world is contained in it, that is the common goal of all religions.'[1] This passage may exceed our understanding, but the more we contemplate images such as this one, the more connections with traditional thought become unavoidable. Meaning is endless.

I wish to explain the connections often drawn in this book between the art work and traditional or religious symbolism. Some of these links are mine, and I

offer them because they seem to me to have a potential to unify us as human beings. But many come from the patients themselves: I have learned that it helps many people to relate their situation to a different order of things when faced with the impossibility of making sense of it in an ordinary way. I hope that readers – of any religious orientation or of none – will allow that we are all capable of questioning our lives in this way; such searching has always gone on, hence the references to seekers of earlier times who still communicate with us through traditional or religious texts.

I have chosen the pictures on these pages to serve as an introduction to the work that follows because this question, 'why?', is present in all of us, as well as being especially potent for this particular woman who was facing the end of her life. It is hoped that they may inspire a feeling of commonality that might be sustained throughout the reader's encounter with the subsequent work.

A similar questioning arose for another woman, who painted three grey-white fluffy clouds like question marks. Evenly spaced against a blue background, they seem to be asking, 'who am I?' She described her painting as *The Cloud of Unknowing*, reminding us of a fourteenth-century anonymous book on the art of contemplative prayer. The sense of not knowing includes not only 'why' cancer develops and 'how' to obtain a cure but, equally important, 'Which way now? Is there a need to change direction in lifestyle or attitude? What does the future hold? How to adjust to the circumstances now visited upon me?'

S omeone finds himself standing at a crossroads with a signpost indicating past, present and future directions. Which way now? As can be seen from this rather painful image, the communication of questions, even when they reach an intolerable level, is made more possible through the image itself, together with the release of feeling which has evidently accompanied the making of it. Many people have remarked that cancer has brought about a turning point in their lives, one that has had tremendous significance for them. For some, a recourse to art therapy has helped by enabling them to ask their questions more deeply and to find a response in themselves, often unexpectedly, from a level where another understanding resides, worthy of respect and cultivation.

The moments of experience depicted here, felt at times of crisis in a life, do not usually continue with the force of their initial impact. People find many ways of enduring their situation, or of dismissing episodes of illness in order to live life to the full. Frequently, however, a new appreciation has been born, leading to a certain inner change that could be said to be one of the aims of human existence. This is what I hope will be conveyed by the art work presented in this volume.

3 *A* starting point
Art therapy for pleasure, diversion and achievement

The sight of a large, new, rainbow-hued box of crayons, trays of transparent pots of paint in a range of inviting colours, a collection of well-used brushes of all sizes – this and more is often the last thing people expect to see before their eyes when they find themselves patients in a hospital. Some cannot believe their luck when they discover that these materials are available for them, but many are nonplussed. What on earth has this to do with them, especially now, faced with the problems of an illness such as cancer? 'No, it's not my thing,' 'I am hopeless at drawing, really I am,' 'I was never any good at school, I wouldn't have a clue what to draw,' 'I can't even draw a straight line.' All these responses can arise, sometimes even mounting to anxiety that they are *expected* to do something. But this is just one way of introducing the idea of using art materials to an unsuspecting non-painter.

It takes time and the development of trust for people to come to consider that art making might have something to offer them. This is especially so when 'art' is viewed as something quite beyond them, done only by 'artists' or by young children in their primitive way. I mention trust because the therapist must fully recognise that she is yet another stranger among many for the patient to encounter. Only by engaging with individuals, with gentleness and warmth, and allowing topics to emerge through conversation that touch their needs and interests can she let them know that she has

time and a strategy which might be helpful if they wish to explore it with her. The therapist is not there to impose, but to open a way for people to find, perhaps, a new experience of themselves apart from their 'jungle of thoughts' while lying in a hospital ward undergoing treatment. Frequently, the first step is to find the courage to have a go, explore the materials, enjoy the process and see what happens, possibly with the feeling that there is nothing to lose. If subject matter is a problem then why not just doodle, play, try to make a picture of the bedside flowers or just copy a greetings card. Anything goes.

A bored ex-civil servant from the Inland Revenue, unable to concentrate on books and not interested in television, made this picture of octopuses and dolphins. She was very interested in archaeology and liked to make embroidery, so it was suggested that she made a design for her sewing using picture postcards of Minoan wall frescoes. Although she had decided that art was not her thing, she agreed to do this, and began a piece of work that was a source of interest and pleasure for her for six weeks. As her illness progressed she became slower in the execution, but finally her sense of achievement gave her great satisfaction. So keen was she on her weekly art session that on one occasion she made such haste that she fell out of her wheelchair! Fortunately, no harm was done.

*T*he very elderly lady who made this flower picture worked very slowly in several stages with great concentration. She made a study of whatever flower was nearest to her at her bedside, and then showed them all together in a single bunch. Her pleasure in her unexpected achievement was great, and she gave the work to a member of her family as a memento.

This woman in her thirties, suffering from advanced breast cancer, had an interest in art materials aroused by her neighbour in the next bed and became keen to speak to the art therapist. She had never been any good at art at school, she said, but she loved colour. Everyone understands that to play a musical instrument well is impossible without years of practice, yet for some reason we feel inadequate if we cannot make a competent painting without any training. This idea was specially interesting to her because she was a musician and understood it very well. She agreed to have a go, and I encouraged her not to worry about drawing but simply to choose the colours that she liked and put them on the paper – they would soon speak back to her and maybe suggest what could come next.

This was sufficient encouragement and she began with reds, which she liked best. She became engrossed in the process; after filling the paper with a red and purple landscape she said how much she had enjoyed the colours. In brief encounters such as this there is no time for any formulation of therapeutic aims. Art therapy can only be placed at the service of the patient with all the possibilities that the process can offer.

This painting was done by an elderly woman with abdominal cancer who came to the hospital every few weeks for chemotherapy. She had been attending art classes and was keen to occupy her time by painting. She also enjoyed talking about art, so we looked at art books together. The opportunity to paint helped her through her periods in hospital, providing a distraction from the treatment whe was undergoing.

$\mathcal{T}$hese two paintings were the end of a long series of work made by a patient in her fifties who was in bed for many weeks awaiting possible surgery. During this time, art became an important part of her life; from very tentative and anxious beginnings her skill developed significantly, and with it her confidence. At one point she suddenly abandoned her careful flower studies and made some paintings like this one. Flushed and exhilarated, she applied paint to paper with a freedom and vigour that were remarkable in one so ill. However, when painting alone in the absence of the art therapist she always continued with carefully observed paintings of flowers, which were in great demand from her family and friends. During the nine meetings we had together, she told me how excited she was about her painting and how releasing and relaxing she found it to be.

When surgery was imminent she was longing to paint, despite being in pain. Unable to sit up, she accepted crayons and a pad so that she could work lying down. She decided to depict a mask, which then became a clown – she said that it must be herself, one hand on her hip, saying, 'Oh well, what next then!' Even after her operation, she had her crayons with her and managed to finish the drawing by adding a bunch of carefully worked multicoloured balloons. Her nurses in the intensive care unit were astonished. She recovered and went home.

Some years later, I learnt by chance that at this gallant woman's funeral her husband had mounted an exhibition of all the work she had done in hospital. Thus art lives on and in this case it was a source of poignant delight and comfort for her family and friends.

Last night, I went for a walk along the river where I gathered shells, grasses and long supple reeds

Now in the morning, I have made a picture with the store of shells, grasses and long supple reeds

*T*hese beautiful felt-tip drawings were made by a young woman with advanced breast cancer, who was originally from South Africa. Reluctant to try anything at first, she wondered what could be in store for her if she made the effort, but decided that since she could not sleep at night it might be helpful. She was also rather inhibited by a neurological problem due to the cancer which meant that she could not use her right hand. She explains that all her drawings were made by a right-handed person using the left hand.

She had been studying icons, and we can see how a feeling for the sacred certainly comes through in the quality of these drawings. They appear jewel-like, and some of them, worked out from the centre, give the impression of a mandala, the ancient Sanskrit symbol of the universe. We established a warm relationship; later, as illness took its toll and she became unable to draw or even to speak, I simply read to her.

Through this series of drawings we sense a spiritual search; maybe the effort that went into them was of help to this patient on her difficult journey. Something that was undertaken simply to occupy the wakeful night hours became increasingly more significant; this is often the case with those who begin art therapy as a means of diversion during long hospital days. Entering a new realm of experience as a result of concentrating their attention with the help of art materials, patients can find something very different from everything else in hospital life. A new energy and interest will then often arise.

The Marico moon is like a woman laying green flowers on a grave

The grave, this patient said, held no terrors for her. It seemed to me that the flowers look rather like mistletoe, the Anthroposophical remedy for cancer.

'I was very tired when I did this drawing and felt bored.
I felt I was repeating myself without care or interest, so
then I took a much-needed sleep and felt refreshed.
Then I further refreshed myself by listening to some
music. Goodnight!'

4 The impact of hospital life

For many people, admission to hospital can be a difficult event; even if it is not a new experience, it is the last place where most of us want to be. For others, however, it can be an enormous relief to know that in hospital they will be cared for and everything will be done to help and treat them. In either case, once there, individuals feel expected to adopt the role of patient – consciously or unconsciously, willingly or reluctantly. They sense the need to be compliant, undemanding, and to accept more or less unquestioningly the pronouncements of their carers, the doctors and nurses.

Since patients quite naturally feel dependent upon this team for their cure, they will do as little as possible to jeopardize relationships. Hospital means treatment, comfort and support; but it can also mean isolation, unfamiliar surroundings, submission to painful or unpleasant and invasive procedures, and a loss of independence and identity. All this must be tolerated as stoically as possible in order not to betray the debt of gratitude, which is very real, towards caring, hard-pressed members of the hospital staff. However, strong feelings about all these factors can arise, and the use of images offers a release to patients who find it too difficult or risky to put their emotions into words. Indeed, good and bad feelings can be expressed at the same time, as quite ambivalent reactions may be experienced.

An elderly woman shows in this picture how mixed is her experience of hospital. Up above the roof in the ward are the patients, prone in their beds, attended in order of hierarchy by the medical establishment. They are accompanied by positive, optimistic words. At the bottom of the picture, well demarcated and held down beneath the pathway, we read the patient's interpretation of her diagnosis. Words have been incorporated into the picture, which perhaps was easier than voicing them.

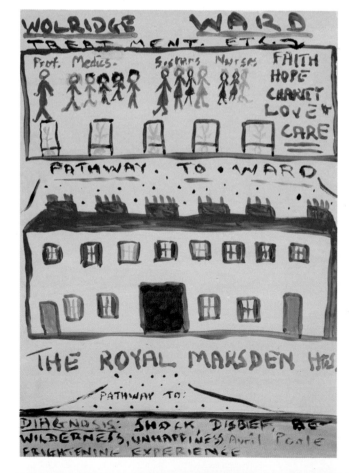

THE BRIDGE OF FAITH.   26·9·91

The Bridge of Faith was drawn by an elderly English general practitioner undergoing surgery; he depicts a bridge on which appear the initials of the hospital. He felt that in traversing this bridge he was enabled to cross from a gloomy situation into a much brighter one, which also seemed to involve some kind of homecoming. He was very diffident about this piece of work, feeling that it was childlike, but none the less he insisted that 'the message was there'. References to childhood often accompany the attempts of those who have done no drawing or painting since they were children when, as likely as not, they were labelled 'hopeless at art'.

*T*he animals in this picture seem more solid than the humans: stick people serve well to depict the nature of this woman's experience. She lies prostrate on an island or perhaps it is some form of raft, for in spite of her separation from the mainland many lines reach out to prevent her drifting further away. She is securely held, presumably by all those who care for her, cats included. She appears to be undergoing various procedures including the use of a syringe; what could be read as a radiotherapy machine is being operated from a boat a short distance away upon which people seem to be enjoying themselves. Beside the patient lies a teddy bear – shock has led to feelings of dependence and the need for a 'comforter' which, in the absence of the mother, is depicted as the toy that is classically the first object of a baby's affection after weaning. The loss of autonomy suffered by this woman seems to have brought to the forefront emotions from her infancy.

From all this we can tentatively infer that although she feels isolated, and has somewhat regressed to childhood in her current situation, this patient does not feel abandoned by family and friends. She looks more like a victim than a patient, having relinquished much of her adult autonomy. Like the cats, the teddy bear, a necessary support, has more solidity than the human beings, including herself. What a harmless but pictorially powerful way of communicating her vulnerability.

*P*art of the reaction to illness and hospitalisation for
this young woman was to feel herself imprisoned
and manipulated like a puppet by the staff who were
caring for her. Here she is falling headlong, perhaps
between the staff, whom she said she also saw as
puppets.

appears from behind her symbol of authority, the frilly nurse's cap. She smiles out of the picture, benign, beautiful and decorative. It is hard for a patient to admit how bad it feels to be deprived of hair and youthful feminine looks, especially in the presence of good-looking nurses.

*C*hemotherapy is a powerful drug treatment that can sometimes have unpleasant side effects such as temporary loss of hair, a disfigurement keenly felt by many people. Its benefits can be equally dramatic, so it is not surprising that this form of treatment is welcomed with mixed feelings. Here, the head of a grinning dog or wolf is attached to the drip stand; the drug is dispensed through its lolling tongue, from which a line is attached to the patient. Is she taking this beast for a walk on the end of a lead, or is she tied to it and trying to escape? It is hard to tell.

In the next drawing, a nurse is pilloried on a drip stand, but she is endowed with luxuriant hair which

THERE IS A PATIENT IN THERE SOMEWHERE

WEDS ON MARSDON KNT

The Wednesday ward round on this patient's unit is notorious for the large numbers of medical people who attend it. I have counted up to seventeen, a daunting prospect for the patient in the bed. What must it feel like to be scrutinised by so many doctors, some of them more interested in your condition than in you as an individual? The doctors on the unit appreciated this drawing and well understood what it was trying to convey.

When I met this friendly young graphic designer she was very pleased to be offered art materials as she wanted to offload some very angry feelings. After ten years of abdominal cancer, she was in hospital having yet further treatment and had just received very bad news about her prognosis. She was in great distress, partly because of this news, but more particularly because of the way it had been given to her. She felt it had been delivered in a very insensitive manner with the doctor asking her, 'Do you want to know the truth, or do you want bullshit?'

Taking a risk, I offered her a very large sheet of paper to stick up on the wall of her room. Unlike many patients, she was at home with these materials, and I thought that perhaps the size of the sheet might equal the strength of her feelings. It was accepted with enthusiasm and then, reluctantly, I had to leave her. When we next met she had covered the whole sheet in paint, the powerful images seeming to have been executed with much energy. She was keen to tell me what had happened. She had painted in two stages and had been exhausted afterwards, but it had been a wonderful experience because she had felt so relaxed and glad to have got rid of her tremendous anger and negative energy.

She described her picture in detail. At first there was just anger and herself in the centre, with violent red brush-strokes radiating out. At the top right is a mass of indistinguishable faces which seem to merge into each other. These are all the people surrounding her – doctors, nurses and so on – only half-known to her. The black and red circular patches with ragged edges are the tumours all around her from which there is no escape; their edges are somewhat eroded by the healing green of the chemotherapy. A large vertical finger occupying the left third of the page is saying, 'Up yours!' – she wanted to send up everything.

At this stage she took a walk, feeling tired but relieved from the tension of her anger. Later, she resumed work and at some point tears appeared, running down the paper on the bottom right side, expressing her sadness. Then more positive aspects began to appear: blocks of purple signifying healing, green and yellow indicating chemotherapy and new growth. She then explained that her body – the image in the centre – was partly veiled in pink to conceal her innermost parts and feelings from public gaze. She did not want everything to be available to be seen by others. Finally, exhausted, she had cried a lot, but felt wonderful for having shed her anger. Wanting to explore her new position, she accepted crayons and a pad so that she could continue working although she had little energy left.

If someone can avail himself of a creative opportunity to this extent it can be a great help. This patient did have the advantage of familiarity with art materials, but on the other hand she had not found it necessary to conceal her desperate feelings behind her technique. Technical skills can be a hindrance as well as a help: an aesthetically presentable piece of work may achieve a response only at the level on which it was made. In this case, however, this young woman's entire life energy was temporarily invested in this painting, far beyond any consideration of aesthetics for their own sake. She was able to use the creative opportunity for her own most pressing needs. How else, I wondered, could she have found such a release and an undoubtable means of communication to those who were witness to her suffering?

As the stories unfold through this book, it will become clear that such physical and mental suffering may be but a stage of the journey for some people, which is often alleviated by expressive opportunity. Patients who feel that they have lost a great deal can still affirm their existence and their worth.

5 The body

Our bodies are the containers of everything we are and through them pass all the experiences we shall ever have. On one level the body is the beginning and the end; on another, it is a vehicle for another body of a different materiality which, according to religious traditions, can have no beginning nor end. It is the visible evidence of our existence – we see, hear, touch and sense our own body and that of another. It is as precious to us as life itself, being the bearer of life. Within it, unseen organs work in the dark without our conscious participation, processing and sustaining everything necessary for existence. Not until the functioning of these organs is disturbed do we become aware of them. We treat our bodies in different ways, value them and rely on them according to the dictates of inherent talents, tastes and tendencies. Externally we clothe and decorate them according to fashion or personal preferences. In health we think we possess our bodies; in illness, particularly cancer, that sense of control is lost.

What is currently known as 'body image' is a deeply felt support for us as social, sexual human beings. It is a picture held inside us of ourselves as we think we are – masculine, feminine, normal, acceptable, presentable, desirable, or not. When surgery is required as a treatment for cancer (especially when its effects are visible exteriorly as in mastectomy or surgery undertaken on the head and neck), the body image is altered and the consequences of this are sharply felt by the patient. Adaptation may be needed. As well as a conscious awareness of a change in appearance, there is also a deep concern about changes that occur internally – particularly the presence of tumours which are often felt as alien, invasive and evil. Hence it is not surprising that images concerning these inner events should appear outwardly in art work, often to the surprise and disbelief of the patient who makes the piece. For some this can be a relief; for others it is disturbing how such images can emerge without their conscious consent. This is where the presence of the therapist can be a support for the patient as he searches for an acceptance on a conscious level of what is taking place in a deeper part of himself. Sometimes the art work may help the patient to come to terms with the changes that are taking place.

When this patient began her collage, she thought she was making a Japanese sun – but then she realised, to her surprise, that it had turned into a breast. She was delighted at her surgeon's interest in the work when she showed it to him. He thought that the cockade was a medal for gallantry and that the purple triangle was her inverted nipple and the area where the disease had been. So, quite unexpectedly, as the Japanese sun was appearing on the paper her body was asking for recognition of the changes that were taking place and a way seemed to open to express them. This helped her to come to terms with her condition: she was then able to remark that breasts were frivolous as well as important.

*I*n a determined confrontation with her illness, this patient addressed her concerns for her body with an unflinching directness and wry humour. Anatomical drawings are overlaid with coloured areas showing lungs, heart and the areas of disease – these are under attack from her mind which seeks to control the situation in this symbolic manner. Mind over body is the motivating force; in the bottom right we see her, strongly affirmed by the double image, smiling broadly with her heart again displayed in the appropriate place.

She attended the art therapy group for two years while receiving a variety of other treatments. As time went by, her painting became more and more related to her situation, each piece of work reflecting her feelings about events occurring in her life at the time. The work increased in freedom and strength. When she returned home to Israel she had amassed a portfolio of work that went with her so that she could mount an exhibition there; her work was also shown in the hospital in London. Her paintings bore titles such as *Looks like a conflict, Joy, Frustration, After the pain, Freedom, The smile.*

When cancer appears in the earlier years of life it is often accompanied by a profound disbelief. One valid way to cope with the situation is to deny the path that science tells us the illness may take. Many people simply get on with life. But, for some, art therapy can help to reconcile this tension that arises between belief and disbelief, and perhaps enable a look in a direction somewhere between the two. So for this woman in her forties, art offered a creative response among many conflicting feelings, something in which she seemed to find healing and, to a certain degree, fulfilment.

The next story again shows a deep concern for what is happening in the body after cancer has appeared. This patient was around fifty, and was suffering from a bowel obstruction after an operation for ovarian cancer two years before. A very courageous woman, she had to accept bad news and the likelihood of more surgery in the near future. Confined to her room, being tube-fed for some weeks, food and mealtimes no longer had any meaning for her. In spite of her poor prognosis she remained cheerful, saying that she had had a wonderfully full and busy life, that she felt very supported by her family and friends and had no regrets about her past. She could even say that she found the peace and quiet of her little room helpful because it gave her an opportunity to reflect and meditate in a way that had been difficult when she had been so active.

She was a physiotherapist, so she well understood her position. She welcomed the appearance of the art therapists, because she did not have much to do during the day and often could not concentrate on reading for very long. However, she maintained that she was no good at painting or drawing and would not know where to begin. We decided to start with collage, tearing and sticking coloured tissue papers, and looked at an examples of what another patient had made the previous week. Collage sometimes relieves the pressure of having to make a 'good' painting and it appealed to this patient, so she was left to doodle on the paper prior to using the tissue.

On my return visit the next week, she showed me her completed work. She was excited by what she had done and amazed at the content of her very colourful 'doodle'. It was begun with no ideas at all, and had arisen entirely unexpectedly. She asked if she could interpret it to me, and proceeded to explain that it described her entire illness. The original ovarian tumour was late in being diagnosed and by the time it was removed it was the shape of a foetus. She showed how the external orifices were depicted; her intestines with all her pain and discomfort were represented in multicoloured swirling shapes. In particular, she pointed out numerous circular forms which represented wind that could not escape and had given her great trouble.

Her consultant showed great interest in the collage, which pleased her. Then she said that it had become 'too subjective', so she stopped working on it. She was so surprised at what had happened that she began to worry about what might appear next. Maybe the work began to pose a threat of revealing more than she could cope with. This collage was an immaculate piece of work: each coloured shape was stuck down perfectly (not easy with tissue paper), one colour separated from the adjacent one by a neat black line, and not a wrinkle throughout. Perhaps a need for control was a part of her nature, and this creation came as something of a shock to her.

After this event she began to paint, tentatively at first, as with the bedside flowers. Gradually she gained in confidence, seeming to find two different styles. On the one hand, she began to make closely observed flower studies, which rapidly improved as she gained in skill. These she made by herself at all hours of the day; they were in great demand from her friends and family, which brought its own satisfaction.

On the other hand, when working in the presence of the art therapist, a completely different possibility was discovered. Provided with a large sheet of paper and a brush, she began to 'splosh', as she termed it. Colours were chosen, mixed and applied with strength and rapidity until the sheet of paper exploded into a flower garden. After this first experiment her face was suffused with colour and utter astonishment at what she had achieved. She immediately asked for more paper and tried again. Two paintings were enough at the first session. Subsequently, we were able to discuss this new-found trust she had found in her own abilities. With support from the therapist, she could now paint without fear of the outcome, not knowing in advance exactly what she was going to do.

The body is central to us at all times, but with such a diagnosis a new valuation of it appears. For the mind, cancer evokes elements of the past and consideration of the future, but the body is ever present in time and in space; it is little wonder, therefore, that changes accompanying diagnosis and treatment have such an impact. These effects should never be underestimated, and acknowledgement of them by the therapist may help.

6 Journeys through treatment

There are moments for all of us when we are impelled to question the direction that our lives are taking. Maybe these moments appear at a certain stage, or maybe they are evoked by events that cause us to stop in our tracks, open our eyes to where we find ourselves and reflect on what we see. This place of intersection – a meeting ground both of our lives in time and of our value systems – is encompassed by questions. Sometimes described as a crisis point, it can be feared or welcomed, or maybe both. Do we find ourselves retreating, are we diverted, or do we resolve to try to find a different way to meet events?

Some say that life is never the same again after a diagnosis of cancer and the treatments that follow. The way back to a previous existence – which, in retrospect, seemed so carefree – is closed. Time and forgetfulness may interpose themselves between the continuation of life and these events, but at this moment an awareness of mortality is bound to present itself, however fleetingly. How to understand this new situation is a question for many people. 'I had never realised how precious life was until cancer knocked on my door,' was the reflection of one woman. 'Circles, circles, going round in circles, is there a way out of this maze?' the question of another. Sheer disbelief was expressed by one person who then went on to express her deep appreciation of everything in her life: 'Is this really me? Am I dreaming? NO. The dark, dark road leading . . . where?'

Some people may use art quite deliberately as a way of coping with their situation, re-evaluating their lives and questioning the direction in which they should go. To reach this stage requires a significant step in acknowledging one's illness and its possible outcome. Not everybody is able to let themselves be so open to their predicament but, for those who can, the process of picture-making can play a valuable part in their becoming more whole.

One young man was in hospital for the first time, newly diagnosed and undergoing surgery for cancer in his bladder. During his stay he made what he called a 'diary' of his experience. He borrowed art therapy crayons and paper from another patient and had already started work when I saw him for the first time. He had completed the first two of a series of pictures which were to depict a very revealing process of thought and feeling. He did not make much use of words within the drawings but he did give them titles, and then took great delight in getting me to deduce what I thought he was trying to say through them. He described them himself in considerable detail as each one appeared.

The Island. This image arose partly from an impression he had retained from passing over islands in a plane, but it also represented his torso. The pond in the centre of the island is his bladder, and the green fish in it were consuming his cancer cells.

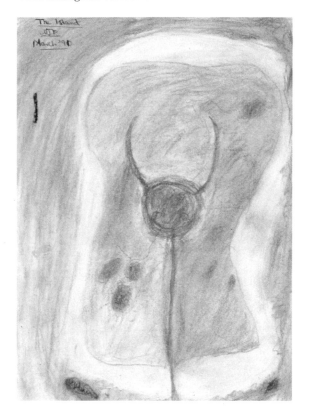

The Family Tree. This picture depicts himself and his family – his parents are the two larger trees in the foreground, and he and his brother are the two smaller trees behind. Roots and branches are intertwined, forming a chalice in the branches which represents the sacrament of marriage between his parents. It also reminded him of the sands of time – but whether for them, for him or for all of them, I was not quite sure. The repeated images of three encircled plants again spoke of his closeness to his parents.

Major Surgery. Two surgeons with wool and needles are 'knitting' him back to health in the form of a patchwork quilt. The surgeons also become conductors of music, surrounded by healing hands and musical instruments. The rainbows represent healing or spiritual forces.

Symbolic Fruit. A richly coloured mango and a banana hang from the same slender stalk; the picture described how heavy parts of his body had felt after his operation.

Crossroads. Two crosses, each with eight branches, are perhaps situated on different planes. Birds, keys and keyholes, small animals, and the healing fish are all part of this complex picture.

Re-birth. In a watery environment, a man in red boxing gloves is breaking out of a golden eggshell and striding out of the picture. The halo indicates some new kind of spiritual awareness. The smile on his face, he explained, could seem fixed and meaningless, but in fact he felt it was positive. Again, the healing fish appear.

This is an interesting series because it describes so fully the inner processes this young man underwent during his illness. The diagnosis immediately brought him to the point of re-evaluating all aspects of his life. First and most directly, there is concern for his body, seen in isolation as an island and with a wish for healing forces to be at work. Secondly, there is his need for and appreciation of his family. He recognises a sacred quality to this relationship, but realises also that it is subject to time passing and is not endless. The encircled triple images seem to suggest a protective quality in his family life. Then his multifaceted body is entrusted to surgeons, surrounded by the healing forces of light, sound and hands – or maybe they are bridging a gap in his lifespan and restoring the continuity that seemed broken by illness? Post-operatively, his attention is reclaimed by his body, the 'fruit' of his manhood being a focus of his awareness and concern. This vulnerability is then replaced by a new spirit of regeneration: one is reminded of the golden egg of Hindu tradition from which Brahma burst forth. Mind over body, he is determined to overcome his illness but not without recognising in the final drawing that there are question marks as to the direction of his future life. Embodied in trees, living questions are doubled to form keys – it seems that he feels himself at a new axis that is derived from an older, underlying one. Through suffering his orientation might change, struggle and choice seem to offer themselves to him – through illness he has gained a new perspective on an existence that previously had gone unquestioned.

It is now seven years since this series of drawings, and the young lawyer recently wrote to me, indicating his thoughts and feelings since that time. His letter is most revealing about the meanings that may have been hidden in these images, and with his permission it is reproduced here in full.

Dear Camilla,
This is to record my thoughts on seeing again the images I drew some seven years ago when last in the hospital. First, the symbol of the fish. I remember we reflected at the time on where this came from. It is of course a Christian symbol, but also I have since discovered it is a symbol of the Jews. I have some Jewish ancestry and when searching for an animal spirit with which to fight my illness, the healing fish was the predominant image.

I was interested in your comment about the golden egg from which Brahma burst forth in Hindu tradition. Before Christianity was brought to the shores of my country of origin, my ancestors were Hindus. Even to this day, Hindus and Catholics live there as neighbours.

About the *symbolic fruit*, I remember your comment when you first saw the picture. You said there was a lot of life there. Certainly if you consider the symbol to represent manhood and sexuality, this is an aspect of life where I do feel an increased enthusiasm, interest and vigour.

Looking back at these pictures some seven years on, I am amazed at how prophetic some of them have proved to be. You mentioned the 'sands of time' in connection with *The Family Tree*. Well, time has indeed taken its toll, and I have since lost my brother and, some two years later, my father. But the image of the trees remains vivid and the coupling of trees now mirrors my brother and father in the spirit world and my mother and me in the earthly world.

But it is the prophetic images of *Crossroads* that strike me most. Here we are seven years on in time. I have returned to the RMH to have two hernias repaired one of which appeared some four months after the death of my father. Somehow I feel these two incidents are linked, the physical rupture manifesting the emotional, historical and physical separation I felt from my father. Now, however, I feel the strength of his spirit inspiring me.

Crossroads was one of the later pictures I drew while I was recovering from surgery. The animal figures and countryside scenes of fences and gates presage the change in direction of my legal career after surgery, which led me to dealing with a number of legal matters relating to farming and animals.

The cats intrigued me. These reminded me of a teacher at school who taught me history and German literature and who was a scout master. His favourite pets were cats and he always started classes by drawing a cat's head in the corner of the blackboard. He himself had suffered from cancer, but was in remission for over thirty years before finally succumbing to his illness. But the event seven years on which this image seemed to predict is the fact of my working with a colleague in the same office on different aspects of legal issues relating to

the same subject matter. He was my schoolfriend in the same class and taught by the same teacher. It was only a few months ago that we were remembering our teacher together. His guiding spirit appears to be nearby.

The books indicate a course of study I undertook part-time resulting in a further postgraduate degree in law. The bible with the tassel across it represents my taking up reading regularly in church after the loss of my brother, something I had not done since my schooldays. Fish and birds were my father's favourite pets. The aeroplane reflects the travelling I have done to far-off places – Australia, the Far East and America. The image of the nun's habit in blue and the girl with the long black hair at opposite ends of the picture symbolise different aspects, both spiritual and sensual, of the woman I have formed a strong attachment to, looking perhaps towards the portals of marriage symbolised by the arch, the wedding arch. I was intrigued by your idea that what I regarded as the nun's habit in blue looks like a keyhole. It may be that this person represents the keyhole in the door to the next chapter of my life.

Last, but not least, the drawing board, which brings me here writing this letter in your art therapy room in the rehabilitation unit of the RMH, seven years on. I remember at the time you thought the picture had a dream-like quality and I could not think of a reason for some of the random images which had appeared, but now I see they were prophetic in nature.

Yours
Z.

A young woman undergoing a course of radiotherapy for abdominal cancer joined an art therapy group in the rehabilitation unit. Her own comments on this painting were: 'These are pathways like the lines in the road. People are on all different levels, up in heaven, going up, and in hell. Two of them are so involved in each other that they are going round in circles. These two have just killed someone. These are standing on each other's shoulders helping each other up. Some are going up, some down. The paths are pink because it represents growth as well as decay.' She added: 'It is busy everywhere, but the art therapy room seems quite different – cut off from the rest, like an island of peace.' I felt that she saw all these characters as being part of her own inner world – perhaps she recognised many different levels of possibility in herself.

One normally energetic and active patient, in hospital for three months after setbacks in her treatment for breast cancer, suffered from shortness of breath and found her physical limitations very trying. During radiotherapy treatment she began to attend the art therapy group and made a number of paintings. She took her initial inspiration from D. H. Lawrence's 'The Almond Blossom':

Even iron can put forth
Even iron.

Connecting this with her recent struggles, she depicted an anvil surmounted by fire and black clouds of smoke – a symbol for earth and matter upon which she had had to submit to being hammered out, subject to forces beyond her control. On the right side is a sickle moon, with blossoming flowers growing again out of the minerals discarded from the anvil:

Strange storming up from the dense under-earth
Along the iron, to the living steel
In rose hot tips, and flakes of rose-pale snow.[1]

'Filling the gap', as she described it, is a snail moving from the anvil and the flames towards the regenerating, flowering earth. Stretched forward from the confines of its shell (into which it can contract and withdraw for safety and immobility), its feelers are extended, becoming a symbol of renewal, like the blossom. In this one painting we can see a rich combination of images, a brave reflection of this woman's path towards a renewed capacity for life, although she still feels herself to be somewhat 'in between'.

In the second painting, the moon has moved into another phase; the snail is again visible, central to the picture, but in the far distance. The light of the moon shows us a hillside covered with trees; a village with neatly laid-out fields beside it give an impression of community. Here are not only echoes from the previous painting but intimations of the next. The area described here as the village occupies the part of the paper which in the first work is taken up by the anvil and in the third by volcanoes. It is a patch of red, like a volcano before it

has erupted. The snail approaches it here, but retreats in the next picture. In the distance we see it making its way up the hill, half-way between bottom and top, and separated from the village by a band of trees. It looks rather small and alone in a large world where communities and their support do exist but are not so accessible or sheltering as a hospital. After three months in the care of a hospital the thought of having to survive in the world outside can seem daunting. We feel the snail has still some way to go.

In the third painting, the moon is in yet another phase. The snail reappears and is again central to the picture but is not quite so remote. Again it seems to be at a point of transition – feelers in one realm, body in another. However, the most striking elements here are the three erupting volcanoes, belching out clouds of black smoke and lumps of lava. Air, earth, fire and water mingle and are transformed in these eruptions, which are a primary force of nature. In some cultures, volcanic eruptions are thought of as dragons embodying both the fire of life and also destruction. What could they mean to this snail in passage? It is just leaving the area at the left described by the patient as one of 'death and sterility', for one where the lava flow with its sulphur and minerals has already regenerated the earth, and life is reappearing all the more verdantly.

The illness itself, the patient's breathing problems, her own inner world, her reference to guilt which she described as a 'corrosive thing', are left unexplained. Who knows what other pressures within this uncomplaining woman may seek release or transformation?

The fourth painting is on a paper plate, circular and containing. A young dragon has appeared, made from carefully manipulated coloured tissue paper. His curved body and tail are not dissimilar to the coiled snail shell. He, too, like the volcano, can emit fire, though now the fire is embodied in flesh. Each foot has five shapely claws – an indication of power in Chinese symbolism. Yet for all his attributes, this fabulous animal seems very small and vulnerable, also playful.

'The question evolves from picture to picture, resonating with the previous one while asking another question.'[2] There is no doubting the connectedness of these four paintings, made at weekly intervals, and the search that they involved. The passage of the patient's life, with its attendant difficulties and trials, can be reflected upon, objectified and communicated to others by means of this work. From these few examples of her work, we can to some extent understand the nature of her experiences. Perhaps for her, as for others, something had changed, so that the 'journey' begins to be understood in the light of the words of Plotinus: 'What then is our course, what the manner of our flight? This is not a journey for the feet; the feet bring us only from land to land; nor need you think of coach or ship to carry you away; all this order of things you must set aside and refuse to see; you must close the eyes and call instead upon another vision which is to be waked within you, a vision, the birth-right of all, which few turn to use.'[3]

*F*rom the artists

We all seek affirmation in one way or another during our lives, and for those who find themselves 'patients' it is no different – in fact, a need for affirmation may increase. For this reason, many people do not wish for anonymity regarding their work, but are eager to be seen, heard and acknowledged in their predicament. Here are the accounts of two patients in their own words.

The Angry Tree

I had been feeling happy and relieved after my mastectomy and reconstruction operation, drawing positive pictures with enthusiasm and humour. Then, a week later, my emotions flared up and anger spilled out into my painting. The tree turned into my body and my legs became roots, giving an aura of complete, 'I'm stuck with this dis-ease!' This is the third time it has returned. Anger from deep within my roots was surfacing, forcing me to ask questions about the cancer. The four angels are drawn into the battle, trying to give me spiritual encouragement and support.

Why does one have to have permission to be angry? Eventually I got into conversation with the cancer and told it that now it has gone it can't come back – or can it? Who is going to win this argument?

Merry Witch Getwell

I wanted to 'tell' everyone not to be frightened of the cancer, operations, hospitals – one can get on top of these situations, be in control of one's body again. The friendly witch is with my little helper (I am sure it is my spiritual help) in disguise as Cat Chemo! I wanted to be a child again, play, imagine I was safe, then be looked after, no responsibilities. There was tremendous joy in working with the tissue paper and colours in this painting, and writing the statement that the Merry Witch Getwell and Cat Chemo can help anyone at any time. This is how I wanted my painting to be. I wanted other patients to view it and feel as happy and encouraged to fight on regardless.

Doing art therapy at the Royal Marsden Hospital was a major turning point for me and my cancer treatment. What was in my head came out in drawings that reflected back to me how I was feeling emotionally. Meditation on a visual level – as I have learned to 'read' my drawings back to myself. I am always astounded at what comes out on the paper, it is almost automatic. The colours and medium have always been important to me as well.

Merry "Witch 'Getwell" and her friendly "Cat·Chemo"... just love to capture nasty cells.

Send them down the 'Hickman' line and ask them to find the cancer... or anything else!!

Witch "Getwell" will then take "Cat Chemo" to a magic place called 'Speedy Recovery' and in no time you will be better♥!!

Tally-Ho! Chemo

Hazel 64·5

During radiotherapy treatment following my surgery I was admitted to hospital a further time for additional psychological support. It was then that I was introduced to art therapy, and it has been a valid part of my recovery not just from cancer but from the traumas that led me there. The memory of my first session is still with me – leaving the security of my corner of the ward to enter a strange space was quite daunting. I stared at a blank sheet of paper that was offered me, quite devoid of imagination. Then explanations given to me about the different materials created a 'spark' and I remember tearing tissue paper into tiny pieces and screwing it all up until I had a heap of colour and texture on the table. That session resulted in a blob of tissue stuck on to the centre of the paper the size of a penny.

It was a beginning . . . From pent-up emotions such as anger, resentment, frustration and pain were born things of happiness and calm, along with freedom and insight a continuing process in a safe space with a group of other patients, yet I was able to express myself as an individual. The sharing is a very beneficial aspect of this. Visualisation and realisation of colour and form can lead to quite a heady excitement or equally to tranquillity.

The day of the 'spark' resulted in an underwater collage with all the fish swimming in the same direction – the picture is symbolic of a certain realisation of myself. It involved many hours over several weeks to complete, both in art therapy sessions and finally in my room on the ward. After reaching out in all directions, I became completely immersed in thoughts and feelings, and there came a growing up and an inward healing. The chaos turned to tranquillity and a sense of direction – the fish seemed to materialise out of nowhere, while I sat on my bed surrounded by tissue paper. I was late for supper on the ward that night, the fish having taken me over.

Looking back, I realise it was reassuring to know there was this safe space in art therapy in which I could dream and explore painful issues without the need for words. There have been many pictures and experiences since then.

Valerie Coffin '98

Flow of Life

My mother died of cancer in July 1997. As a young woman, she was given the Sufi name of Hiavarti, meaning 'flowing water'. I did this drawing over three months while mourning her death. It is her energy that I am experiencing in the drawing. I had no conception of what the picture would be when I started – it just emerged as I worked. It is very symbolic of her life – she was a wonderful seamstress. I can hear her voice when she was teaching me as a child about cutting fabric . . . you cut it according to the way it falls, fabric like water will always find its own level.

The fallen branch has diverted the waters, but they have all fallen in the same pool. The trees on the horizon are so familiar – they seem to appear like signposts in my work. It helped me a great deal to express myself pictorially in that time of grief: words were inadequate. I will treasure this picture always in memory of my mother.

7 *M*emories and reflections

Memory! What is this strange function which can relate us to impressions and experiences from the past recorded somewhere in our brains and in our bodies? What are the strange pathways memory offers that lead us from the present into the past, and what deep meanings can it supply for those who find themselves in the unfamiliar environment of a hospital, cut off from their usual sources of meaning? In this situation, to evoke memories may inwardly restore a sense of identity that has been seriously eroded. Who is this person confined to bed, for whom all points of reference that gave meaning to daily life are now absent?

Over and over again in art therapy, patients find memories arising as they begin to make pictures – sometimes happy, often poignant, always significant. No art work, however seemingly understated, minimal, bland or simple, can be dismissed because it may appear naive, if the patient recognises where the image comes from. We should never underestimate the strength of meaning and feeling behind these statements.

*I*n this simple rendering of an old man's garden, with a barely discernible cat basking in the sun on the shed roof, there is a clear idea of what mattered to this patient and what he was missing while in hospital.

This patient, a single social worker in middle age, was in hospital for weeks and very limited in her movements due to the position of a tumour. Feeling too unaccustomed to painting to attempt it, she began instead to make a collage from coloured tissue paper. To her surprise, what emerged was the main object of pride and affection in her life – her dog. We see them together in a rather compressed and precipitous gap between earth and sky, going for a walk and playing with a ball. Since her dog was large and beautiful, she used him for collecting money for the blind, and related with pleasure how succesful he was at the job. Her collage, together with the photographs she then brought in, made it feel almost as if the dog was with us in the hospital. The memory of him brought meaning to her at a bleak and difficult time as she shared her thoughts and photographs with the rest of the group.

A farmer's wife with recurrent lung cancer told us of the 'mad' year she had had with her husband when she had first been diagnosed. She could no longer climb the hill behind their house to fly her kite as she had done in the past – her picture of this memory helped her to speak of the sadness she felt.

*P*atients frequently find themselves making pictures of some idealised place where they would like to be, living the perfect life of peace, good health and contentment. The image which seems to answer this need is often that of the country cottage, with thatched roof, roses round the door and smoke coming out of the chimney indicating life within. Sometimes it is set in a cosy garden, sometimes in the hills. It is an understandable dream when the reality is a hospital bed, harsh strip lights, strangers, medical procedures and noise.

The same patient followed that example of an ideal place with this interesting image of a long straight path disappearing into distant hills, with tall trees on its margins. Birds, sometimes considered to be the messengers of the soul, are flying in the distance where the trees end. Perhaps this patient recognised that the ideal character of the country cottage did not correspond to her situation, much as she might have wished it, and that she still had a further journey to make.

These drawings of the East African coastline were a
memory from an Asian woman's childhood. It is
hoped that by being able to give form to these happy
recollections through art, she tempered her present
situation in hospital far from home.

*T*his young mother, twenty-six years old, had advanced abdominal cancer. It was clearly important to her to try and bring something of her home life and its meaning into her hospitalised existence. She had a son of eighteen months, and there were difficulties within the family regarding his care. From our first meeting she was keen to try painting, so I left materials with her. When I returned she showed me her work, pleased because no one could understand what it was that she had painted. She described the image to me as a drain in the road surrounded by a puddle of oil like a rainbow. I found this quite a threatening image, with the heavy kerb leaning over the drain, yet the presence of the rainbow puddle somewhat redeemed it. It seemed that this painting embodied her fear of the unknown, yet she may have felt supported by the rainbow colours. It may be significant that in Jungian terms, red pertains to feelings, and blue to spirituality.

Her subsequent paintings treated matters that were dear to her. First, a corner of her baby's room with his clothes and shoes neatly arranged. Her child was only brought in to see her from time to time, and she missed him a great deal.

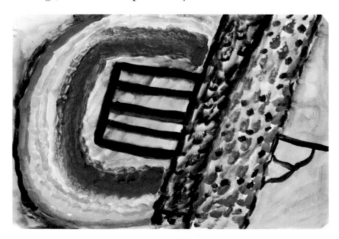

Secondly, the food she would like but was unable to eat due to her illness.

Thirdly, a figure clothed in blue, kneeling at what seems to be an altar rail, which she painted in order to help herself find 'a prayerful attitude'.

Fourth is a painting made by her partner, the father of her son. His inscriptions on it express his attempts to sustain hope in himself and his little family.

A portrait of her partner.

A place in the sun where ideally she would like to be.

Later, in the rehabilitation ward, she resumed painting, but it was of a less personal nature. She enjoyed contributing to a new book of art work for the ward, decorating the cover and making a carefully observed painting of tulips – she was extremely proud of this, because they were so realistic, saying, 'I really tried with them!' When short of ideas, she derived great pleasure from copying a postcard of a storm at sea by Turner, and her work was much admired. After major surgery she spoke to me of dying, with a childlike simplicity. I read her poetry from a book she had been given. One of her last remarks to me was, 'I am sure that up there they will all be painting, doing art therapy!'

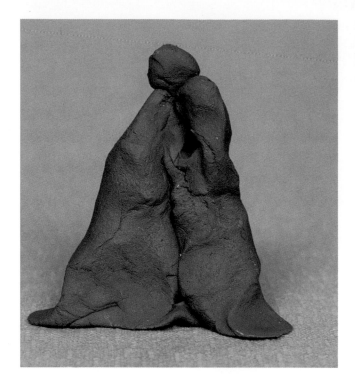

*T*his patient, retired and living overseas, had
received succesful treatment for her cancer in the
hospital, but the ordeal had temporarily left her feeling
physically reduced and emotionally delicate. After
trying her hand with painting, she discovered a greater
feeling for clay and rapidly made this series of small
coupled figures. Away from home, feeling rather
distanced from her ailing husband, and carrying painful
memories of a lukewarm relationship with her mother,
she revealed in these poignant figures a deep longing for
loving, meaningful contact.

The small pieces, with little
discernible detail, have a
distinctly devotional
atmosphere – more so in fact
than some modern sculpture
found in churches. They might
be related to certain sculptures
from thirteenth-century Italy –
work with a quality of the sacred
which comes through clearly after
many centuries. Between the figures is an
extraordinary intimacy – as between
mother and child, lover and beloved, even
teacher and disciple. Taken together, these
individual pairs evoke an intensely
personal, yet universal, human feeling of
love and devotion. We are left with an

impression that this woman, who enjoyed a sociable
expatriate life in Spain, had unexpectedly touched a
part of her nature that acknowledged a need for a deep
and intimate relationship with something or someone
which was beyond words.

Major surgery leaves most people in a very sensitive
state and more open to the emotions. Feelings reside
closer to the surface and are very easily evoked. This
can make ordinary life quite difficult to resume, yet
often such different psychological states are appreciated
for a while. It seemed both natural and interesting that
this patient was keen to own the figures she had made.
The deeper levels in us seek to be acknowledged and
will persist, in spite of the denial that is also in us.
When the time came for her to leave hospital, she took
the figures home with her.

It is evident that those who come to art therapy following treatment for cancer frequently bring with them outstanding emotional problems from their entire lives preceding the onset of their illness. The illness can be a watershed from which individuals look back, re-evaluate their lives and also question the future direction to take. These impulses may pass, but while the questions and the memories are still pressing, art therapy offers a means for their exploration.

We can begin to appreciate now that art therapy as offered in a cancer hospital is far from merely a useful tool for assisting diagnosis. It is not used for prognosis, analysis or corrections of the patient's situation. In its best sense, it is a vehicle for increasing understanding and a channel for the expression of unspeakable concerns. These examples have shown that a sense of meaning can be rediscovered through image-making and assistance can be found in discovering a new orientation towards what has to be faced.

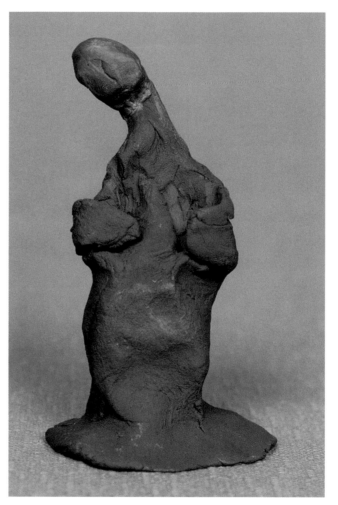

8 *P*ain and change

Total pain. Psyche inseparable from soma.
Beyond words, aside from thinking
Pictorial images can communicate
both to their maker and to another
deeply sourced resources.
Much has been lost, seemingly nothing gained
but a new strange set of values
through uninvited inescapable affliction.
Time available is precious.
Can something else be understood?

Anyone who has had cancer and has been through treatment would agree that any physical pain was only a part of the experience. Many say their lives are changed, and that, among other strong feelings, anxiety and fear are evoked – feelings arising from the psyche that are also painful. Physical and mental pain can directly influence each other; they can increase the total experience of suffering, acting in a seemingly vicious circle. Science approaches the relief of physical pain through pharmacology, but the psychological aspects are underestimated even today. Here the arts therapies can have a major part to play, although their outcomes are difficult to evaluate scientifically. The art work described in this chapter played a significant role in alleviating not only the psychological but even the physical distress of these patients.

The first example, the outcome of a single session, illustrates in particular the close link between psyche and soma, and the dramatically cathartic effect that can be obtained. A retired and very successful businessman came to the art therapy group while in rehabilitation recovering from recent surgery. He had lived with cancer for eighteen years and had undergone surgery on very many occasions. Wanting to make a birthday card for his grandson, he started to make a charming picture of a running deer-like creature.

After a while he began to experience considerable pain in his chest and it became difficult for him to continue. I asked if he would be willing to try an experiment; he agreed, and I placed a clean sheet of paper in front of him. I asked him to try to be open to the pain rather than to tense himself and close down in the face of it, then to see if he could allow it to take on a colour and a shape and to put this image on the paper. With little hesitation, he picked up a large brush, chose red paint saying that the pain was very hot, and made a red ragged patch on the sheet. As he focused his attention on the pain, it diminished, so he then covered the red with a cooling blue. As he did so, the pain moved to the other side of his chest, and a second red area appeared on the paper. From there it moved to his spine, the area of his recent surgery, but again it diminished in the chest and he covered it with blue.

Suddenly, he began to have breathing difficulties

The first occasion on which I met the next patient, she had just been admitted and was sitting cross-legged on her bed in the ward, frightened and in pain. In her early forties, she had been struggling to treat her cancer for a year using complementary methods; in spite of her fear of hospitals and treatments, she had eventually acknowledged that she needed more help. She was so distressed from pain and anxiety that sedation had little effect; at this point, someone suggested calling the art therapist!

and walked to the window for air. Again I encouraged him to relax and after a few difficult breaths he found himself overcome by uncontrollable weeping. After a few short moments he recovered himself, explaining that this had happened before and was nothing to do with the pain but was connected with the love that he felt from his wife and family. The pain, however, had gone, and with it the breathing problem. A moment later he was called to see his doctor, so he left the room abruptly. I heard subsequently that he had recounted this event to the doctor, saying what a tremendous release he had found in the experience. Whatever the emotional pressures upon him, the link between them and his physical distress was undeniable.

This is a very direct approach to the problem of pain. The experience of others may not be so dramatic, but undeniably their pain can be helped in differing ways.

When I found her in this state I cut introductions to a minimum, and suggested that we immediately embarked on some painting. Choosing a large brush and loading it with paint, she began covering the paper in an energetic, unrestrained, disorganised manner. After a while, pausing to draw breath, she remarked that it was 'chaotic' and asked for a second sheet of paper. Already something in her had changed, because she began by

next, at the top of the painting, she added symbols of those two traditions – the cross, and a stupa surmounted by radiating marks suggestive of energy. Below was a strange combination of shapes in strong blue, which represented herself. The black was the cancer and on the right, in brown, what she described as a protective hand. She indicated quite clearly the meaning of all these colours herself.

All was now no longer just pain and despair – healing elements were beginning to be discovered. Certainly her pain had abated and in herself she was composed and more at peace in her situation. Her medical attendants were impressed by the change that had occurred in her through this encounter with art therapy.

painting the blue spiral at the bottom left with a care and concentration that had been absent from the first painting. The inner space was then filled with magenta, green and more blue. Next appeared the black road stretching from side to side, bifurcating at one end as if two possibilities existed that led in different directions. Then another blue shape arose on the opposite side of this dark way, partly surrounded by the strong light of yellow, which was repeated on the other side within and outside the original blue spiral. Further red was added, as if pain and suffering were still there. Then in thick white paint a 'bridge' leapt over the black road linking the blue areas of paint. Finally, more considered and seemingly healing touches of magenta were added in carefully selected areas, touches that I felt had some significance. Her title was indeed *The bridge*.

Asking for a third piece of paper she began again, in yet a different frame of mind. First, slashes of green appeared up and down across the page; these were then interspersed with the magenta of the chemotherapy drug, depicting the treatment she dreaded so much and which she had tried to avoid at all costs. Brought up as a Christian, she had lately adopted the Buddhist view;

The young man in his early twenties who made this drawing was alive and well five years later, but at the time he had been made aware that he was unlikely to survive a recurrent brain tumour. In the knowledge of the eventually happy outcome, we may feel less shocked that in this picture he was depicting his own funeral. He had begun the work by experimenting with paint and brush, but found that it did not enable him to say what was uppermost in his mind. He turned instead to crayons, which enabled him to draw and write what he could not speak. I knew – and he knew that I knew – the anguish he was experiencing. When he had completed the work, he still felt a need to apologise for his overriding concern, and all he could say was, 'I am sorry, but that is just how I felt.'

An initial outburst with the paintbrush was followed in this work by a pencil drawing of a family group – mother, father and child – protected and encapsulated in gold and green sun-ray strokes of colour. As well as shock – an inevitable accompaniment to a diagnosis of cancer – there was a sudden abrupt awakening to an appreciation of what life meant, at heart, for this young woman. Central to her was her relationship with her husband and child, but also a new valuation of her own life during each passing moment. Shocks of this kind can produce, if even temporarily, a new awareness. Sometimes this is sustained, leading people to value each and every small thing in their daily lives, with even ordinary things acquiring a new significance.

This rather haunted face gazes numbly past us. The words are strong, but the image is stronger.

*I*n a flower-bedecked world, sunny but not cloudless, we see a well for water. Appearing over the edge, only just visible, is the top of a head and a pair of hands, which are gripping on to the edge of the well for dear life. This person expressed with despondency the thought that every time she managed to start climbing out of the well she was knocked back again. There seemed to be no hope of ever regaining a place in the world of sun, trees and flowers that lay around her. These feelings could be communicated to and acknowledged by others through the drawing, although nothing could be changed. Here is a situation where, as so often, the therapist can but 'attend, witness and wait.'

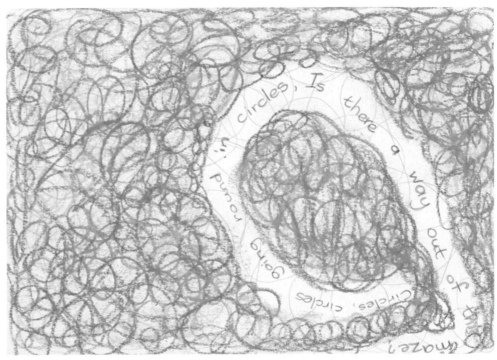

*A*nother powerful image of frustration at the repetitive, unending nature of this person's illness.

*O*ne must be tentative in approaching someone who is very ill, but a person's mood cannot be judged by their outward appearance – many times a strong need for an expressive outlet has appeared even in very incapacitated patients. So it was with this woman. I approached her with care, half-expecting to be sent away, but she seemed happy to talk, recalling at length her life as a teacher. She said she would like to have a 'splosh' with the paints, so I set up the materials for her to use in her half-lying position. To my amazement, and that of other patients nearby who were aware of how ill she was, she rapidly gathered strength as she applied paint to paper with increasingly confident movements, until after a quarter of an hour she had made a bold and beautiful painting of flowers in a vase.

She attacked a second sheet of paper, covering it with red and black crosses and swirling circles, surmounted by what looks like a crown. Lying back, she exclaimed, 'Phew, that's better!' She explained that she had started gently with the flowers, then the vase to give it a firm base, then put black on the tips of the flowers to balance it. With the second painting she felt different, and she scrabbled on the paper with her fingers in frustration as she spoke. 'I really had to beat this thing and felt very angry. Now I feel much better for it and just want to sit.' The next day I visited her but she was too weak to speak. I learned a little of her circumstances later and realised how much she had needed this one opportunity to pour out her pent-up feelings.

*L*osses can be many and painful and they occur in different areas of life. Perhaps one of the hardest to live with is the loss of the ability to speak, which accompanies some forms of throat cancer. The natural voice can be replaced by mechanical means, but it must be extraordinarily difficult to live with these problems. The middle-aged man who made these drawings had suffered not only the loss of his voice, but also his ability to work, his girlfriend and the possibility of pursuing his hobbies, one of which had been playing the trumpet. He was suffering from chronic intractable pain and was very angry at what he perceived to be the failure of the surgical team to alleviate it. He was unable to sleep well or swallow easily. He was at his wits' end when he began to draw, asserting that art was not his thing and he had never done it before.

He began with a vase a flowers, carefully and strongly worked. It was a theme that he repeated several times during his stay in hospital and the drawings were given away as gifts. He felt loss of meaning and purpose very keenly, and he seemed to be affirming the fact that he could achieve something that was valued by others.

He then turned his efforts towards drawing motor-boats, well lit and sturdy. He liked to describe how he used to enjoy taking his friends out and that they all used to play music together on board.

On another occasion he drew a cottage deep in the country where he would much rather be than in London.

The table-tennis player has no ball and no opponent, as though he has not been given even a sporting chance.

His despair and agitation mounted until one weekend he was overwhelmed by anger at his situation, and likened himself to an aircraft being shot down in flames.

After this traumatic weekend his life evened out a little. Now the aircraft is intact and maintaining its course, although the sky still appears unsettled.

Again the motor yacht with its well-lit interior is coping with a restless sea. He described, through written notes, how he felt that he had been treated badly by life in recent years and in particular by some people, especially officialdom. He felt a great lack of support and friendship, which he ascribed to his illness.

A powerful black bird is apparently threatening a terrified smaller bird, hovering over a glowing rosy apple floating on the sea below them. Poised above the apple neither can enjoy the fruit, so transfixed are they by each other. The patient identified himself very definitely with the smaller bird. We feel acutely how the apple, symbol of all desirable earthly things floating in the sea of life, was being denied to this frightened bird who could only stare into the eyes of the bird of prey, which was perhaps a symbol of his fate and the cruel blow it had struck him.

When he felt that the time for drawing had passed, this patient wrote to his doctor saying how much it had helped him to 'direct some of his awful thoughts on to paper, and that although they had no artistic value we could see what they were supposed to be.' He had also found it good to write and to try to talk about them.

It is hard to read this story without a sense of dismay at the suffering that this patient endured. However, the bringing into being of images from the wordless realms of the human psyche to be shared by an attentive other, maybe also wordless, can offer a sort of release which is difficult to define.

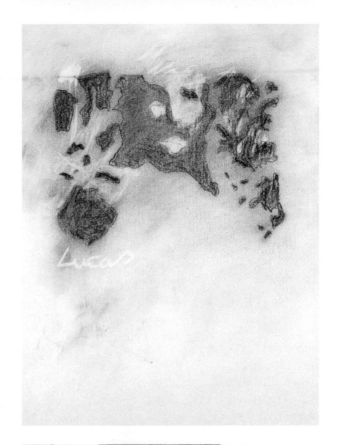

This young man in his thirties with cancer of the lymphatic system was not only searching for a meaning to his suffering, but also wished to communicate what he could of it to another. He had undergone much treatment over the previous months, was confined to bed and in pain. When I made his acquaintance initially he asked for a pad of paper and some crayons. On the next visit he showed me the work that he had done, asking me to identify his images. The first was a strangely fragmented black and grey drawing, part of which began to reveal itself as a face or mask. A mouth and one eye socket were identifiable, the rest seemed to be shattered and blown apart. Describing it as 'the face of the suffering Christ', he began to talk about his suffering, the impossibility of communicating its reality to anyone, and the isolation he felt as a result.

He showed me a second drawing: the same image, but enlarged and reinforced by being drawn in red. He talked at length about what he was going through. Perhaps he could give some meaning to his affliction by identifying himself with the sufferings of Christ; to relate his condition to something of a higher order was vitally important for him. I hoped he had found a direction approaching the statement of Simone Weil: 'no pain, however great, up to the point of losing consciousness, touches that part of the soul which consents to a right orientation.'[1]

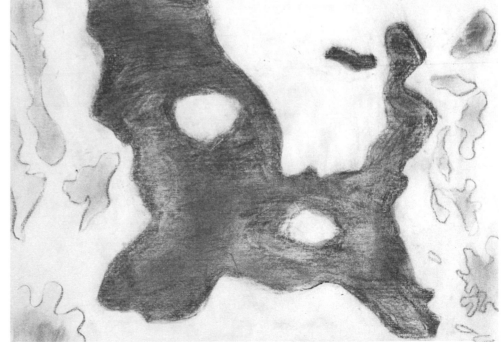

*L*astly I include in this section a painting by a young woman who knew she was dying. She said that the making of it offered her enormous relief. I have seen very few statements as powerful as this: both words and picture combine to leave us in no doubt that she would not 'go gentle into that good night'.[2] (The camera at the foot of the painting indicates its size.)

'Learn thou to suffer and thou shalt be able not to suffer.'[3] Pain is seen as a frequent concomitant of an illness such as cancer, and pain is something that we suffer rather than invite. The word 'suffering' has mixed connotations, one of being subjugated involuntarily to unpleasant circumstances, and another which is active in its import. It is possible to infer from this injunction of Christ to his Apostles that this capacity to suffer can be acquired actively, through some sort of effort or orientation on one's own part. This is not easy to understand, and maybe it can only be understood when brought about through unavoidable circumstances. However, both aspects can be present together. As human beings, the event of suffering pain takes place in both psyche and soma – total pain suffered by the individual alone, often in the absence of any bridges offering the possibility of sharing it. What hope is there of communicating it when it is so intimate and has such an isolating effect? What is its meaning? If life has seemed a meaningless event then suffering, too, is meaningless. If, on the other hand, life is experienced as having meaning through whatever channel or tradition, then suffering is part of life and therefore has significance. According to Simone Weil, suffering is 'a divine educational method.'[4] Whether recognised or not, the question is how to search for a right

orientation, and by what means. Responses are many and varied, but these images have shown how some people have found a way to share their pain, both psychic and physical. Art therapy helps people to find a 'safe' way in which to obtain relief – through it they can avoid any subsequent feelings of remorse or fear of retribution. Remorse is for burdening others, especially family and friends, to whom the patient is anxious not to appear ungrateful, nor to hurt. Fear of retribution can exist in relation to the carers upon whose support and care the patient relies: anger, criticism and doubt cannot be voiced easily in that direction. It can be difficult to find a way to relieve the pressure exerted by strong feelings such as shock, fear, anger, loss and frustration – feelings that do not correspond at all with the widely held ethic of 'positive thinking', a tyranny that besets many people, not only the patient.

Some of these pictures may seem gloomy or tragic, but they were the result of an unfamiliar and unexpected opportunity to engage with art therapy to communicate feelings that were otherwise initially too strong for mere words. Displacing them on to a piece of paper by means of images which can be viewed and discussed makes the matter less subjective. A degree of blessed separation from the overwhelming nature of their situation can then be experienced by their makers.

9 Search and affirmation

In the extraordinary theatre of life that is this hospital, the great and uniquely human impulses of hope, faith and love begin to emerge in the art work of many patients. Feelings of this nature naturally begin to assume a new significance for many people, who refer to the discovery of hope, the rediscovery of religious faith, or an awakening to the experience of love in a new way. I have therefore linked them with the idea of search – search for something that was lost or buried or, at any rate, that did not feature very strongly in everyday life while it proceeded in a relatively normal fashion. For many, the 'catastrophic' event of cancer enables them to stop and reflect on the direction of their lives to an extent that can quickly come to be valued at the expense of many other things.

In ancient Greek this word 'catastophe' meant an overthrowing or a sudden turn; in drama, the turn of the plot. An apparent calamity offers something quite unexpected – and it is exactly this that patients often acknowledge. A statement such as 'it may seem strange, but I am actually glad I got cancer!' may seem extreme – but we cannot know what depths of understanding a patient may reach by means of this dreaded experience. Many patients express an appreciation of a new set of values and, moreover, the opportunity to express them and share the feelings involved through the art therapy process. Relief and gratitude are often voiced. Words can be found more easily with the help of a picture to relate to; something has been externalised and becomes, for that moment, more objective. Sharing and empathy can follow from others, who are similarly situated and who are also conducting searches in their own individual ways.

In art therapy, the image becomes the vehicle for this journey into the human psyche towards a source of help. This help, perhaps initially perceived as external, gradually becomes more interiorised. Deeper resources are then discovered and brought into being. Direct or indirect links are sometimes made with traditional symbolism as embodied in the Christian, Jewish or Buddhist faiths, for example, or even in the ancient art of alchemy. 'Archetypal' imagery (as it was termed by Jung) can appear, embodying features that respond to the needs of the patient who portrays them. Jung offered an evocative explanation for this term when he wrote: 'The archetypes are the forms or river-beds along which the current of psychic life has always flowed'; in addition, he defined them as 'impersonal collective forces'.[1]

The therapist, although deeply involved in what is happening, is to a certain extent an outsider. She cannot presume to understand fully what is being experienced, for she herself has not been there, but she has the privilege of receiving at first hand a pictorial rendering of what it might mean. These encounters evoke deep respect. The therapist's task is to attend, witness and wait. She provides the conditions through which the process can be given form, and should try not to hinder it through inappropriate insertion of herself, her own ideas or conditioned responses. She should be open, receptive, supportive and containing for the duration of the contact with the patient.

This series of four felt-pen drawings were part of the search of a young mother with advanced and incapacitating metastatic breast cancer to find help in all the significant imagery she could think of. Very anxious, she found this the only activity she could undertake.

A well-lit church, with a particularly solid roof and steeple, stands with its door partly open; it is approached by a winding path. Perhaps a place of sanctuary and a source of comfort and meaning, the building is centrally placed on the paper. A green tree to one side looks somewhat like an onlooker; many people feel a strong connection with trees, and often use them as a form of self-portraiture.

Secondly, images and words appear, including the fish, all of which relate to this patient's Christian faith, leaving us in no doubt of her call for help.

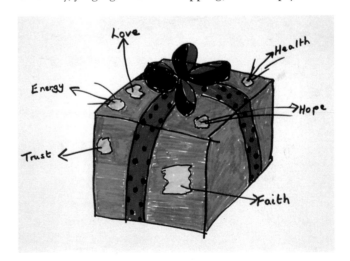

Next is a gift-wrapped box, with the contents clearly marked on the exterior. Were these things she recognised had to be given and could not be bought – or certainly, judging from the wrapping, not cheaply?

In conversation with this distressed young woman I learned that her overwhelming need was for peace from her tormenting thoughts and feelings, so that she could relax. Again we see the cross, single and central to the picture, enhanced with flowers and fish. Her truly difficult situation may have been alleviated by her very prolific image-making of significant symbols.

His second painting was of a golden-handled net submerged in a blue sea. Did he feel trapped in the net, or supported by it in a sea that threatened to submerge him? Again, the meaning is ambivalent but the strength of feeling is clear.

I BELIEVE IN GOD   I BELIEVE IN OTHER THINGS

*T*he two declarations beneath two arching images were made by a wealthy man struck down in early middle age by an incurable form of cancer. He was utterly amazed at what had overtaken him, despite all his hard-won worldly achievements. He told me that he had 'got it all wrong'. We receive an impression of ambivalent feelings from this picture. Although belief in God comes first in the general order of things, belief in 'other things' is much more substantially enshrined in a heavy gold background. Was he struggling to sort out his priorities?

The carpet of prayer. An elderly lady undergoing chemotherapy depicts herself distended by the fluid in her abdomen. She is lying on a carpet, held aloft by her family and the members of her church whom she knew were praying for her. Interestingly, the carpet just hovers above the supporting hands. She was very shy about her religion, but having made the picture was able to talk about it more easily to those who commented on the work as they passed her bed.

Grace from above – undying love. By her own account, this unequivocal and unashamed depiction of an outpouring of grace expressed what this patient actually experienced one night while lying in her hospital bed. Overcome by what had happened, she wished to communicate it to others. She made three identical versions of this image, giving one to the chaplain, one to her nurse and another to the art therapist. Her joy at receiving this gift was still with her when I met her several years later, back in hospital for more treatment.

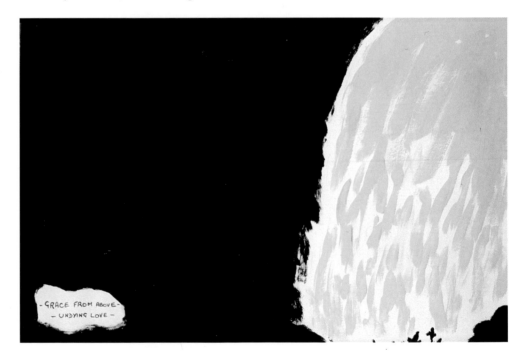

This intriguing picture of a little Buddha, as his author described him, was painted by a young woman while participating in a group art therapy session. She worked hard and attentively for some while, and when it came to her turn to speak about her work she told us how important this figure was for her. Years before she had attended a type of group meditation session, and this Chinese figure appeared for the first time in her field of awareness. She had never been able to re-evoke his presence, until this particular afternoon. She was delighted that she had re-discovered him, or he her, and felt that he was a source of support to her in her time of need. She did not think she would lose contact with him again, and took the painting away, intending to keep it carefully. She stressed that the golden light surrounding the figure was also significant. This patient's own testimony indicates how she had found for herself in this way a source of support that she could trust.

My legs are free. This small drawing by an elderly lady communicates a certain joy and hope. After losing the use of her legs, she had become able to walk again following radiotherapy.

*T*hese two pictures are the work of an extraordinarily courageous young woman faced with recurrent and incurable cancer. This was a patient whom I regard almost with awe because of the manner in which, recognising her situation, she lived with complete inner dignity and yet with a vibrancy of life much loved.

Towards a new dawn. Here she described how she is setting out with her horse, without fear or, as she then added, 'almost without fear'. Much work went into this painting.

She described her second piece of work in this way: 'I spent all afternoon gently using the colours, it was really lovely being able to do it all afternoon. When I am at home it is always mundane things I get caught up with. Opposite me in the side ward a woman was dying and when she had died her husband came over to me and wanted to talk. He said it was an "aura" that I had drawn: I hadn't thought of it like that at all. He asked what I was going to put in the middle and I decided on a figure – I suppose it must be me. I wanted it to feel you were tipping over the edge of a space.' When I remarked that there is much that we do not understand, she responded, 'Yes, life is wonderful, and that understanding comes in bits.'

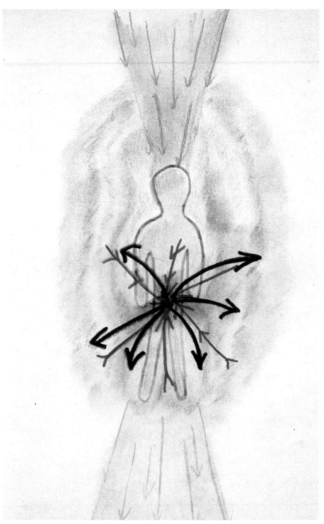

The final two pictures in this chapter express again the three impulses of hope, faith and love. A cottage in Scotland, surrounded by heather, is where this patient would ideally like to have been. Recognising its impossibility, she then made the very powerful second image in which her inner resources are revealed and given form, while not denying the overwhelming wish to be rid of her cancer. This intimate and personal piece of work enabled her to acknowledge to herself and share with another the source of her strength and then talk at length of what it meant to her. The red and black arrows leave us in no doubt about her concern for her body. But she was equally keen to tell me about the aura of light by which she felt surrounded. Of greatest importance was a living,

dynamic energy that she could sense from above whenever she had enough privacy to make herself available to it. This was undoubtedly her greatest source of help, and I could only wonder at her capacity to devote herself to such a real transformative process. Not an ordinary hope or blind faith, it was a real knowledge of the power of an energy that passed into her from above.

10 The tree: a theme of life

'. . . *for the tree of the field is man's life*' (Deuteronomy 20:19)

The depiction of trees in this chapter seems to show a deep acknowledgement that we are part of a structured and living universe. The impulse that leads to the making of this particular image seems to have both subjective and objective qualities. A tree does not argue with the laws that direct its existence: it conforms in every detail, yet it contains a great generative and regenerative force. So it is with a human being – particularly one who through suffering has been brought to the recognition that although he can no longer ignore the circumstances visited upon him, he can still feel something in his nature stronger and more sustainable than a physically ailing body, something that perhaps can be subject to transformation.

Throughout history the tree has been invested in the myths and rituals of many cultures. In many so-called primitive religions it symbolises the axis of the cosmos, the 'world tree' – by climbing it man can ascend to the heavens and be enabled to reach God and transcend the human condition. Numerous myths tell us of human beings coming from trees: Osiris, for example, the Egyptian god of resurrection, was found within a giant tamarisk which had been cut down and used for the central pillar of the palace of Byblos. In the West, we refer to the 'family tree', so the tree also takes

on the aspect of the tribal mother. From Genesis we are imbued with ideas surrounding the tree of life and the tree of the knowledge of good and evil. For Jacob, the tree takes the form of a bridge or ladder between heaven and earth. The cross and the sacrificial tree are symbols far more ancient than Christianity. So a tree is the image of the centre, of life, of rebirth, of knowledge, of evolution, of ascent, of sacrifice and of fertility.

In psychological language, this tree of life can become a metaphor for our own process of maturation – in Jung's terms, 'individuation'. He found in his study of dreams that the tree appeared more frequently at critical periods of life, 'when there was a pressing need for a supporting image of growth and integration.'[1] Before considering each image, some comments can be made about them as a whole. The purpose of art in a therapeutic context is that patients address themselves through imagery, which helps them to contact parts of themselves that are seeking expression and of which they may not be aware. Those parts then speak through the image, regardless of whether they make themselves clear to the reasoning brain or not. Technical skill and artistic standards are unimportant.

An illness such as cancer can strike at the very core of a human being who is then constrained to acknowledge the threat to his physical existence. It would seem that the archetypal symbol of the tree offers itself from the depths of the psyche, representing an entity of which the physical body is but one part. From the pictures, it is possible to deduce that this body is also a vehicle or container for other energies, other possibilities. Sky and earth, above and below, also figure in all these pictures, but it is the tree as a link between the two that is all-important. In each image it is a strongly sensed presence, an undeniable affirmation of life to which the patient is unusually awake because under threat. These different pieces of work, all made by women in their middle years, are strangely similar in detail. All use strong colour and all seem constrained by the boundaries of the paper.

This woman, of independence and strong religious convictions, had an inoperable tumour on the base of her spine which was gradually reducing her mobility and giving her much pain. As with so many people, art was an unfamiliar activity to her; her first piece of work was a collage, a method often found to present less of a challenge than paints. To her surprise, she found that she was depicting herself taking her much-loved dog for a walk.

At the second session she felt enough confidence to use paint and crayons. She made what she described as a 'Winnie the Pooh' world, enjoying the opportunity to paint in a childlike manner. The painting seems to represent much of her inner world. The sturdy tree with its branches lopped off was herself 'mauled' by her illness. A small figure flying a kite was also herself, with a surrealist balloon-flying cat beside her. Birds are in flight behind them. Fish swim in the river and ducks are on the pond, there are rabbits and a dog. Flowers bloom and the sun is just visible in the top right corner. It is a joyful scene full of all the vivid impressions of childhood.

She worked carefully on the white owl sitting encircled in the tree trunk, but said nothing about it.

To the Greeks the owl was sacred to Athena – because it could see in the dark, it was a symbol that united the three qualities of wisdom, knowledge and prudence. Furthermore, it 'stays awake all night to signify the human soul which is never lazy, always in movement by its very nature, which is immortal.'[2] In medieval Christian monasteries it was taken as a sign of meditation, since it remained all day in a hollow tree; it became 'the symbol of the light of the Holy Spirit illuminating the dark soul of the unbeliever.'[3] But it also had less appealing connotations of darkness and death. To symbolise isolation and loneliness, the Psalmist compared himself to 'an owl of the desert' (Psalms 102:6). We are left with the feeling that this bird was indeed a poignant and profound exposition of this patient's inner world.

*F*or this painting of a red tree the patient wrote her own account. 'Art therapy at the hospital began for me about five years ago. It was the day after my mastectomy operation, and I painted a bowl of flowers. In other circumstances I might have hesitated to put paint to paper but there was no question of your being expected to produce a work of art, and I needed to respond positively to what seemed a rather negative situation. Becoming a patient can make one feel passive, and I learned that through painting I could express my own sense of identity.

'Later I was to return for radiotherapy treatment in my hip bone; I welcomed the opportunity to paint and have someone to talk to. I was feeling fragile and really appreciated the security of being in hospital. As a mother I am used to caring for others, but it was good for me then to be cared for and allow myself to be very upset, away from the possibility of worrying or distressing my family. I wanted to be strong for them, but first I was to indulge in a little weakness! Through painting and with the therapist's support I explored feelings of conflict, anger and sorrow. To look at oneself in a mirror is vanity, but for me those glances of reflection helped me to get things sorted out in my mind and go home with some good resolutions. It was autumn and I found myself painting a tree with all the brightly coloured leaves falling from it. Looking åt it I realised that *I* was that tree, with a knot in the trunk (my cancer), having to let go of all those lovely leaves! Then I thought that, once cut, that knot would become an attractive burr veneer valued for its intricate pattern, and I felt comforted. Perhaps through suffering it was possible to become beautiful inside.'

*N*ext we look at a woman in her forties being treated for breast cancer; she was not of English birth and felt particularly isolated. These trees can almost be translated into human figures, bearers of a range of powerful feelings.

'My chemotherapy was due during Christmas time. I felt so emotional, Christmas in hospital! Everyone is having the time of their life and I am shut between four walls, with hardly anyone to talk to. Most patients have left to spend time with their families. In hospital I had a strong feeling of Christmas – tree, bottles of wine, everything generous – but I felt lonely. The art therapist came round with two boxes of crayons, felt-tip pens and a drawing pad. She left them for me in case I felt like using them, but drawing was the last thing I wished to do really. On Christmas Day a friend rang which cheered me up a bit, but still my spirits were low. Suddenly my eye caught sight of the crayons and the pad: should I give it a try, what should I draw? I really can't draw, I had nothing to draw from anyway. I picked them up reluctantly, looked out of the window – nothing inspiring, very few trees. I got out the bright colours and started. I got carried away, not realising how time was passing – I felt calm and relaxed, my thoughts were happier. I felt I didn't need anyone, I was happy on my own with my colours and crayons. People passing by in the corridor must have felt my self-sufficiency. I didn't feel lonely any more in the room on my own. My mind and emotions were occupied for the time I was drawing. I didn't think about my pain. I was as if in a different world.'

In the first of a series of eight extraordinarily vibrant drawings, of which three are shown here, we see a sturdy black tree-trunk central to the page. Rather tenuous leafless branches reach out towards a vivid orange sky; steep and brightly coloured hills converge behind the tree whose roots seem as tenuous as the branches. A pair of black birds fly in the distance. But here again, as in the first picture, is a nest or hollow containing what could be small birds – its position is near the top of the trunk, which would be somewhere in the chest region were it a human figure. Since this patient was of Middle Eastern origins, it may be appropriate to quote Hafiz, a fourteenth-century Persian lyric poet:

On the holy boughs of the Sidra
High up in the heavenly fields,
Beyond terrestrial desire,
My soul-bird a warm nest has built.[4]

The next tree has quite a different quality.
Reminiscent of the willow, its branches incline towards
the earth; they conceal, protect and shelter like a
curtain. The first tree to produce its new leaves in
spring, the willow may here be indicative of a need for
some sort of refuge.

In the third picture, the tree fills the page from side
to side, its seven branches surrounded by a yellow light
that envelops the trunk as well. The whole gives the
impression of a candelabra with seven arms,
reminiscent of a menorah. Again, we see a black knot
or burr on the trunk, there is a red hill in the
background, and moisture seems to fall from the
underside of the tree. Much is suggested by this image –
the candelabra is a symbol of spiritual light and
salvation, the number seven is of infinite significance.
The tree could also be a sort of container or chalice.

This sturdy single tree was painted in a group session by an editor with a recurrence of her illness. Centrally placed, the tree bears dense leafy boughs hardly confined by the limits of the paper. The space in the trunk is arched like a doorway and at a level easy to enter. The members of the group were very interested in this painting, especially in the significance of the empty space. The artist said she had decided that what lay behind or within the space was unknown, but that it held an attraction for her and she was not frightened by it. This invitation to enter more deeply into herself, for that is what it felt like, might offer her some new understanding of her troubled outer life. She seemed very happy with this piece of work, as if it had shown her a possible direction.

This is a very different 'tree', the axis of which was the event of breast cancer for this patient; it was diagnosed over Easter, which made the festival doubly significant as expressive of sacrifice and renewal. Along the bottom margin is the context of passing time: 'life – now – death'; above the axis, or trunk, an open eye occupies the highest point. 'Branches' of coloured tissue paper fan out diagonally from the centre, each branch designated with contrasting attributes, negative on one side, positive on the other. The single eye, with its oval centre, appears to embrace all in its gaze – all the named experiences are seen.

A counsellor and therapist in various fields, this patient had been undergoing radiotherapy for several weeks. She felt unsettled and uncertain about the whole experience, and was trying to find meaning for her life; at the end of a difficult period of treatment, she was wishing to find her way once more in her profession. We were talking by a window and saw that a tree outside, usually insignificant, had broken out in a mass of yellow, pendulous blossoms – a sight that she received as tremendously life-enhancing. It immediately became her theme for painting that day, and for several moments she was transformed, working with vigour and delight, and appreciation for the tree itself. The following week I received this poem from her:

GOLDEN LABURNUM TREE

If I close my eyes
I can see today
An empty room
With a silent ray.

Where I silently lay
With silent fear
Not knowing if
I should be here today.

But today I am here –
If I close my eyes
I can silently see
Rays from a golden Laburnum tree.

A breath away from the empty room
I can now forget the fear and gloom
Joy and spring are silently here
In yellow Laburnum, radiant bloom.

The last two trees show all the human possibility for transformation with the approach of what we call 'death'. They were drawn by a teacher in her fifties. She had visited a cancer help centre which offered art therapy, where she drew the first of two trees. It is grey and leafless, with its branches twisted and even contorted; one small shoot near the ground still retains its leaves. The knot, or wound, that we have seen in the other tree pictures has a clear significance: three red drops fall from it earthwards. The roots are strong and plentiful, and a large sun appears behind the bare branches. We can sense strength, suffering and hope, and also a call for help.

We met four months later when she was receiving chemotherapy treatment, and I discovered that she sustained an extraordinary attitude throughout her illness. Her second tree, her penultimate piece of work, reveals great changes. The colour scheme is completely different, softer and brighter, and flowers grow out of the earth. The bleeding wound is healed, leaving only a

slight scar, but the small branch of hope has gone. But so, too, have the tenacious roots, which seem to be releasing themselves from the earth, and the agonised contorted branch.

The focus of interest is now located in the upper part of the branches, developed with jewel-like blues, pinks and purples. This, the strongest part of the picture, seems to suggest that life now lies in a higher realm and that it is possible to be released from earthly constraints, beautiful though the world is. She seems poised between above and below and ready, even eager, to make the transition. This tree was followed by her last work, a vase of flowers, which she drew the day before she died. Why the choice of flowers on the last day of a patient's life? What were the deep animating forces, and were images more fulfilling than words? She can have had only very little energy at this point, and she must have devoted it to this final gesture. It seems an extraordinary resolution.

11 Rites of passage – Atalia's journey

This chapter is devoted to the work of just one patient, which symbolises her journey through the late stages of illness. She had sustained an interest in painting through numerous hospital admissions; and in the last series of four pictures, made the day before she finally lost consciousness, we can see a process of transformation apparently occurring. Material certainly seems to be lodged in the subconscious of which we are unaware and which is of a universal nature.

An analogy can be made between such images and the ancient tradition of alchemy, 'the great work' as it was sometimes called. A popular misconception holds that, as a precursor of chemistry, alchemy had as its object the transmutation of base metals into gold. In fact, 'the mysterious doctrine of alchemy pertains to a hidden reality of the highest order which constitutes the underlying essence of all truths and all religions.'[1] The doctrine was conveyed in many pictorial symbols as well as texts; four stages existed in the transformative process, each with its own characteristics. From the beginning of her art therapy sessions, these and other symbols of a Trinitarian nature appeared in the work of this woman. Jung reminds us that 'the symbol is not of course an external truth, but it is psychologically true, for it was and is the bridge to all that is best in humanity.' He goes on to say: 'Although we naturally believe in symbols in the first place, we can also understand them, and this is indeed the only viable way

for those who have not been granted the charisma of faith.'[2] If we can temporarily abandon logical thinking, the images that follow may offer us an unexpected encounter with an alternative vision of life. 'In this realm the fixed meaning of things comes to an end.'[3]

Atalia, an Israeli aged forty-two, had recently come to the UK as a 'student'. She had been ill for ten years, and had undergone bilateral mastectomy, chemotherapy, radiotherapy and finally ovariectomy. She then refused any further chemotherapy, followed a macrobiotic diet and used homeopathic agents, but widespread illness caused the collapse of her cervical spine. This improved with radiotherapy, and she was referred to palliative care for pain control.

My contact with Atalia fell into two periods. When I first met her she was making her presence felt on the ward in the only way that seemed possible for her, being demanding, critical and manipulative. She liked to be in control of her treatment and would alter her own medication. Her fighting spirit was extraordinary. She had spent all her life in a kibbutz in Israel with her parents: it had been completely stifling, she said, she had never been allowed any sort of initiative, was always left in the background, and had to wait to be asked before she could do anything. She considered it a wasted life, but eventually found the independence to break away and come to the UK. She was always anxious about her immigration status, fearing up to the last that she might be sent back. I began to understand her desperate need for attention, and her determined though counter-productive attempts to affirm her own existence.

I supported her and encouraged her to make her paintings, giving her my undivided attention when I could, although not unconditionally. Atalia was quite unconcerned about her artistic ability, so she could paint without any fear in that respect. She had done some art therapy previously and considered that, as with most things, she knew all about it. She expressed satisfaction in her ability to handle materials and in her organisational skills – she used morphine cups for mixing paint! At this point, she had no interest (or would not admit to any) in why she painted the images she did, and had no wish to discuss their significance. I accepted that what she painted embodied sufficiently her inner drive towards life, but I regretted that she could not direct more of her energy in this way.

It is interesting to note some points about the style in which Atalia worked. The paintings are powerful; the density of colour shows her intensity and concentration. From the strength of line and movement in the images it is clear that the work is vigorous, in spite of her considerable physical limitations. Nothing is tentative: she worked right up to every boundary of the paper in every painting. Despite an apparent naivety of style, these are sophisticated images, rich in symbolic content. The paper can scarcely contain some of them – life was a big event for this woman and she was not going to let go lightly.

Pomegranate 2. In the second of this series of three, the sun blazes from the top left corner on a sturdy, inclined tree, symbolic of growth, regeneration and inexhaustible life (for more on tree symbolism, see chapter 10). It is leaning towards a flame, in the centre of which is a strange face. The Greeks represented the spirit as a gust of incandescent air; to pass through fire was symbolic of transcending the human condition. On the right, in dark blue within a watery looking area, the pomegranate reappears, larger and more significant. Its shape is reminiscent of a retort, a vessel which in alchemy was also known as the 'philosophic egg': substances were heated in it for a long time to obtain their transformation. So this painting depicts the four elements of earth, air, fire and water.

Pomegranate 1. In this picture the image of a pomegranate is small and does not occupy a very prominent place. There is a wild, almost desperate, feeing in the brush and crayon marks, as though the trees are battling to stand up in a gale. The pomegranate seems to shelter, half-buried in the ground, the storm sweeping over it.

Pomegranate 3. The pomegranate has expanded and looks more like an egg which is bursting out from the top in a shower of colours that Atalia described as like a peacock's tail. The whole image is barely contained by the paper, yet the boundaries are carefully respected. Both these images – the pomegranate and peacock's tails – symbolise the blending or reconciliation of the multiple within a unity or totality, and it is significant that they are juxtaposed in one work. According to Jung, the peacock is an early Christian symbol of the redeemer, second cousin to the

phoenix. A peacock rising from a retort was used to illustrate alchemical manuscripts, as in this eighteenth-century example shown on the left.[4] After ten years of prolonged illness, Atalia depicts her life in the image of the egg, with all its contents, the fruits of her struggles, bursting forth.

The development of the images through these pictures, including her manner of painting, made me wonder if something was beginning to change in Atalia. 'Symbols are not signs or allegories for something known; they seek rather to express something that is little known or completely unknown.'[5] Was there a deeper level in Atalia where these correspondences were significant?

The river. In this strange and rather haunting picture, a river crosses the page diagonally and a cypress tree bisects the composition almost completely. Flowers and butterflies can be seen and a path runs along the river bank. Unlike the previous three pictures, the compositional movement here is from top left to bottom right. Traditon has always bestowed certain attributes to left and right. In the Egyptian system of hieroglyphs, to enter is to move towards the right and to go out is to move towards the left; the right side takes on implications of birth while the left acquires an association with death. In experimental psychology, movement from left to right is also deemed to indicate the passage from unconsciousness to consciousness.

This painting seems to have some ambivalent aspects. The river seems to represent a torrent of life energy, and the flowers and butterflies give an impression of life and beauty, if transitory; the word *psyche*, in ancient Greek, meant both butterfly and soul. On the other hand, the cypress tree is a powerful and ominous presence, cutting as it does right across the stream of life. Swans and fish are also imbued with significance. Atalia did not wish to talk about the picture, but put it on her wall with the others so that it could be seen.

The head of golden hair. In the last of this series (paintings made during her earlier admission), we see the full face of a woman, surmounted by an amazing mass of golden hair, filled with flowers. Springing from the centre of her head, the hair encircles the face on either side, more or less filling the paper; the neckless, disembodied face looks out from underneath. If hair represents energy, then a full head of golden hair even more so, with its symbolism of the sun as a source of life and energy. This picture also seemed to show the presence of tremendous animating forces in Atalia, and she acknowledged that it had much value for her. At this point she was discharged, but we resumed work together when she was re-admitted five months later. Although she was even more reduced physically and quieter in herself, her painting was as strong as before, and even freer.

Mexican desert painting. Atalia's remarks during the course of this painting make an important point for art in therapy. She asked for a small sheet of paper, but seemed content when I framed an area within a larger sheet with masking tape; after this she requested the tape every time, indicating the area she wanted to use. I too liked the tape, finding that I could express my

need to support her in holding the picture within a contained area in this way. In the main I offered an involved but silent presence, to give her maximum space to paint as she would, and when she wanted to talk we talked.

First she painted the background. While painting the threefold image in the centre she said that when she was painting with me she never knew what she was doing and did not care what people thought; when she was at home, she added, it was quite different – there she had to make something look as real as possible so that people would know that she could draw. The painting she did with me was 'definitely not art.' This was an important statement, implying that to produce work free from the usual preconceptions of what art should be like it had to be done in a context where these strong attitudes could be relinquished – i.e. in a therapeutic setting.

She referred to the triple image in the centre, between the two spiky cacti, as the therapist. Did it represent a reconciling element between masculine and feminine parts of herself? What about the dark, rather pendulous sun above the round cactus? The heron/stork image, bringer of life, in the bottom centre? The desert representing the wilderness and domain of the sun? This picture has been remarked on by some people as being hot, hostile and scary.

$\mathcal{T}$hese two pictures were made by Atalia at home; they are what she called 'art' proper.

thought the figure at the bottom right represented. I found it threatening but withheld any comment, and she then said that she thought it was fear, and that the image on the left seemed like some sort of conflict. I pointed out that the birds and star seemed to have quite a different quality. Atalia then said that she thought the picture was mixed in what it expressed, and I wondered why someone should work like this. I pondered over the painting, wondering about birds as symbolic of the soul, about stars or suns, and the strange figures below which gave us both similar feelings. The circular forms were slow in revealing their possible symbolism, then I recalled that when Atalia depicted a tree in other paintings it was usually in this same position on the paper, and I turned my thoughts to trees.

The tree of the soul painting. Atalia, now confined to a wheeelchair, was utterly despairing and spoke of her 'horrendous fears'. There is a feeling of space in this painting. The foreground is occupied by two strange figures. On the left, in two interlocking columns of three, are a series of circles, each enclosing a radiating figure like a flower or the spokes of a wheel. The whole image is surrounded by a fuzzy area, a sort of pink fog, which Atalia worked on very carefully. The figure on the right is a legless or spineless creature with one eye. Above are high-flying birds and over the circular forms a sun is emitting powerful rays.

When Atalia had finished, she asked me what I

The figure by William Law (from the work of Jacob Boehme) depicts the 'tree of the soul' (right) Three circular forms are surmounted by the 'light of Majesty': 'A beam of light from the world of consciousness pierces the "dark world" of the unconscious in which the tree of man's spiritual and psychological development is rooted. Passing through the "fire world" of suffering and experience it opens out in the light of greater consciousness towards the light of God.'[6]

The prayer painting. This was the penultimate session. Atalia's mother had arrived from Israel and was present at the beginning; as usual, there were many interruptions including a long visit from the dietician. When everyone had left the room, she said to me in her now small voice that she would like to disappear in a puff of air, it would be so much easier for everyone. As she painted she spoke about her nightmare situation, her loss of freedom, her fear of having to return to Israel, her mother, the hospital and so on. Gradually the painting developed – the background, the carefully depicted plants, the birds whose shape is heightened with white, and the tree which Atalia described as substantial and protective.

As she was painting in the light in the top left corner a torment of self-questioning began. Why was she so negative, as her friends had told her? Why could she not stand ignorance in others? Why was she still reacting to other people's stupidity? She seemed to recognise in the core of her being a need to change, in particular her impatient and judgemental attitudes towards others. How could she change, she asked? I was about to say that maybe we cannot change ourselves, we can only ask for help, when a moment later Atalia

painted in the three figures saying. 'It's like a prayer.' She had come to this by herself, through painful conversation and self-questioning; I was glad that I had not anticipated her understanding by responding earlier, and was surprised that our thoughts had been almost simultaneous. I put the painting up on the wall, hoping that it would remind her if she was again in difficulty.

I was reminded of the idea of the 'sun door' at the world's end and the tree or pillar by which it is reached. This universal idea appears in many traditions – for example, in the sacred Sanskrit Upanishads we read: 'He reaches the Sun, it opens out for him like a hole in a drum.'[7] The Egyptians had a sun door, which was square, reached by the ladder of Horus. And in the New Testament we read, 'I am the door, by me if any man enter in, he shall be saved' (John 10:9). So I felt that in her final depiction of the supplicant figures, Atalia had for a moment touched on an attitude that might be appropriate for the next stage of her journey. It was also important to acknowledge the impression that these figures seem to be performing a joyful dance, as if in celebration of life. There seems to be a strong similarity with *The ascent of the blessed*, part of a triptych by Hieronymus Bosch (right).

The last four paintings

The sea picture. The last time Atalia painted it was for two and a half hours in one afternoon during which she made these four paintings, sitting in her wheelchair with everything arranged as close as possible. She poured the paint for the first picture straight from the pots; abandoning brushes, she used her fingers. She made desperate movements, but still exercised judgement and care. The sea is turbulent. The thick red paint was applied from the top downwards, so although the red could be read as an explosion, it was also a plunging into the deep. 'The sea is the symbol of Nirvana, and just as Meister Eckhart can speak of the "drowning" so the Buddhist speaks of "immersion" as the final goal. The final end of every torrent is the sea . . . Opposites and likes pertain to the waves and not to the sea.'[8] Eckhart writes: 'Plunge in – this is the drowning.'[9]

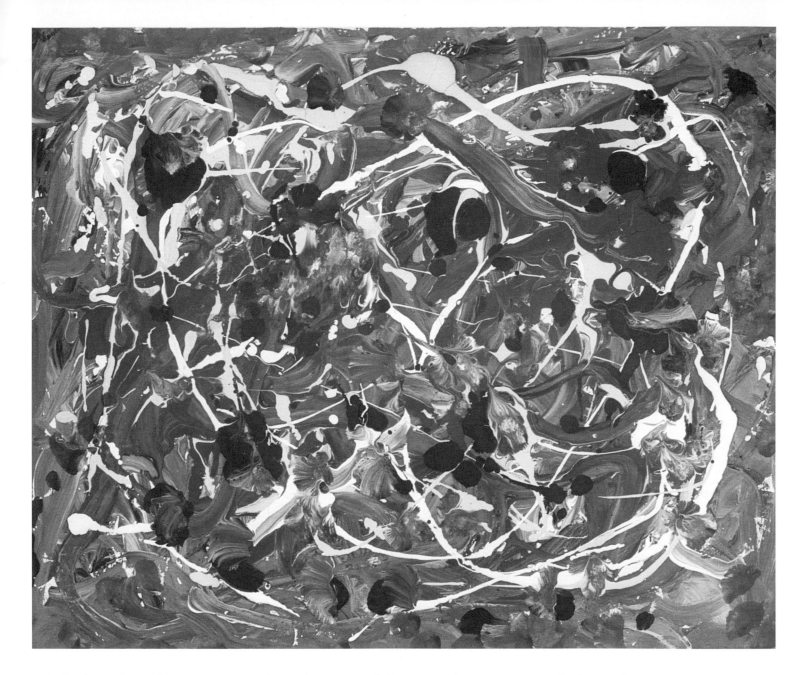

Is this chaos? Again the paint was poured straight from the pots over the paper. Stabbing it with a brush in one hand, a handkerchief in the other held to her eyes as she wept, Atalia asked repeatedly, 'Is this chaos?' It is carefully focused within the paper, however. She seemed reluctant to finish this painting and added paint upon paint, finishing with white. Among many definitions of the *prima materia* – the basic substance of alchemy which is subject to transformation – is that it is the psyche of man. According to one authority, 'Chaos' is one of the names for the *prima materia*.[10] So it would seem that this troubling experience was but a stage in the transformative passage that Atalia was going through.

The pink and yellow painting. In the painting that immediately followed a new stage appeared, one of emerging from chaos and approaching a totally different new realm. Painted from bottom left to top right, a golden path emerges from darkness into light; Atalia referred to it simply as the 'arising of peace and light'. It seems as though a journey to a higher realm was taking place, helping Atalia to endure and redeem her suffering.

Desert with three plants. Atalia asked for another sheet of paper and started on her fourth and final drawing, and what appeared was a complete re-ordering and reintegration with a Trinitarian symbol of totality: 'a threefold cord is not easily broken' (Ecclesiastes 4:10–12). It seemed that something in her was not contemplating 'death' at all; far from indicating a fading away, the paintings seemed to suggest the opposite. For this last picture Atalia asked to use the wax crayons, because they were 'quicker'. She cleaned them carefully before she started, as if purity of colour could bring purity of meaning. Everything in this picture is in threes. The desert landscape has three elements – sky, earth and plants; three plants occupy roughly the left-hand third of the paper. Vertically, it is divided into two parts sky and one part earth.

Something seems to be being distilled through these four pictures – a plunging, a chaos, an arising of light and peace leading to a triple image, the inner structure of unity. At this time, although Atalia did not speak to me of dying, she was obviously declining. But at the same time her painting was sustained in spite of all outer disturbances – the process seemed untouched and unstoppable. I felt that she needed increasing support, to try to allow for this mysterious process that I hoped brought a new understanding, an inner growth, when all possibilities of physical improvement seemed out of the question. Her psyche needed all the help it could get to fulfil its purposes up to the last possible moment, and I wondered how she would have confronted this process without art therapy. These pictures evoke a certain response in me, so how strong can the impulse have been that enabled them to be brought to light in Atalia? On the last occasion I saw her, it was as though she had entered a new stage through the painting. This seemed to be a sort of miracle, if not the sort that she had never ceased to hope for. She died a week later.

12 Poetry within art therapy

As I recall the times when I have read poetry with patients, undeniably the event was nearly always a source of psychological nourishment, both for the patient and, incidentally, myself. When reflecting upon what to offer someone whose life has been narrowed to the point where it seems that everything that made that life worth living is now denied, it appears that the influences that can be transmitted by art, literature and music can be of profound help. What is often aroused by these means is the patient's own capacity for responding to an innate and finer area of perception within himself, so that he can touch a deeper understanding of the direction his life is taking.

I vividly recall listening to a patient speaking at length of her incomprehension and despair at her situation, and trying with her to find a way through it, but to no avail. I then offered her the anthology of poems that I always carry with the art materials.[1] She took the book out of my hands and opened it at the sonnets of Shakespeare. Then she began to read aloud, sometimes repeating lines, sometimes altering them. At once she seemed to find in them a correspondence with her situation, and she wept as she read. She continued with a poem by John Donne, which also corresponded, and finally with 'I am' by John Clare. She was nearly unable to finish it, for the depth of feeling that it aroused, and then said, 'Perhaps this, all this, is me, perhaps this is what I need to understand.'

It had been impossible for her to get out of the thought patterns produced and reinforced by her physical distress. An ordinary verbal exchange between us could not bring new light: I was unable to enter her situation and understand what she was experiencing. The poetry, on the other hand, could immediately touch her, expressing her feelings more closely and vividly that she could herself. It actually illumined them for her, enabling her to realise that she had been rejecting her current situation and that perhaps she could try, at least momentarily, to be open to it instead. It was obvious that no amount of normal conversation could have brought her to such a realisation. Suffering can render people much more sensitive to the inner content of works of art or literature – particularly, it seems, if they are shared with another. The words of Shakespeare, Donne and Clare had, as she voiced them, released her from her torment of that moment.

It is now quite natural for me to move towards this art form if and when an individual no longer wishes or is able to draw or paint. Once a genuine relationship has been established between therapist and patient, poetry reading can offer another related path for exploration and expression of feeling. Much is spoken about improving or maintaining 'quality of life' as an aim for the multidisciplinary care team, but when all the skills have been offered on the level of physical and even psychological care, a patient can still be left bored and in a vacuum, starved of the sort of impressions which feed our deep psychological need for meaning and which provide material for thought. Energy may be very low and capacities reduced, but below the surface the desire for some sort of fulfilment can still be there. Is it enough to leave a patient with pain under control, and physical and social needs addressed? Can we not also help in the voyage of exploration that may urgently need to be begun or continued?

One patient in his fifties, originally from the Caribbean, was physically very incapacitated; confined to a wheelchair and unable to coordinate his hand movements, he did not find it easy to draw or paint, but then his interests were not in that direction. He had been educated in his home country in the traditional colonial style, and was well versed in history and English literature. Sitting in the ward week after week he was desperate for a quality of interest that he could not find in the daily hospital routine, and he had become increasingly silent and uncommunicative.

The occupational therapist and I found ourselves in close collaboration – she visited him frequently, taking him out of the ward in his wheelchair and sharing long conversations with him. I responded to his literary interests by offering him the anthology of verse. He seized upon the book and read, recalling all the poetry he knew, including 'On His Blindness' by Milton and 'The Holy Sonnets' of John Donne. We read aloud to each other in turn, his voice often shaking with emotion as he read. I saw him over several weeks, and after a couple of visits he began to choose and read aloud poems on the subject of death. I introduced him to the poems of D. H. Lawrence, including 'The Ship of Death'. This patient never actually spoke about dying, but this was an inspiring way of exploring his deep feelings about it.

At a late stage, when painting was no longer possible for her, I continued to visit a young Malaysian woman, lying in bed with barely the strength to talk. When she saw the anthology, she recalled a 'tiger' and 'daffodils', so I read Blake and Wordsworth to her. Then she remembered 'water, water everywhere', but instead of 'The Ancient Mariner' in its entirety I chose D. H. Lawrence's 'The Snake'. It has a strong visual quality and also expresses a certain sense of scale – qualities I search for when choosing what to offer to a patient, for a sense of scale is often forgotten when difficulties seem insurmountable. After I had read the poem, the woman opened her eyes and whispered, 'It's not often that poets write about egoism.' This remark, so unexpected, was evidence of her high degree of awareness and sensitivity – she was clearly able and maybe needed to respond to communication at the level offered by the poem.

Another patient, a lecturer in drama and religious studies in her mid thirties, was in hospital for treatment for cancer of the throat. She had attempted a drawing but seemed to find it an effort, and I wondered if poetry reading would be more welcome. When I arrived, her mother and husband were with her, as they frequently were, but it was apparent that I was welcome and she indicated that I should stay. Conversation was extremely slow since she had to write everything down, so I simply put the book in her hands for her to choose something. She marked four poems by D. H. Lawrence. The three of us read them to her in turn, then her husband and mother chose one each from their own poetry book, and I too chose one. All the poems were direct and strong, and an intense atmosphere was created in the room (a nurse who began to enter backed out rapidly). The patient seemed gratified and pleased; her relatives were deeply involved and likewise seemed glad at what we had done. It was a very moving episode.

Poetry can communicate very directly. Visually, in the sense that it creates word pictures, it can be a great ally in stimulating imagery which can then be translated to paper with paint and crayon. Hence it can enable painting to start when previously the process has been blocked. This occurs both with 'artists' and 'non-artists'.

The poetry box
For some years I have used a collection of Japanese haiku, written on index cards, to help patients to find an image from which to paint, an idea I was given by a colleague. Soon after starting it, new contributions began to appear in the box among the original verses: patients coming to the group were writing out favourite quotations or composing their own short verses, and the collection has since grown steadily.

Haiku are a traditional form of Japanese poetry, stemming from several cultures, including Taoism, Confucianism, Buddhism and Zen. Short and succinct, their impact is immediate. 'Haiku is not only poetry, that is a representation in words of the real world; it is a way of life, a mode of living all day long. . . . It is the apprehension of a thing by a realisation of our own original and essential unity with it. The thing perceives itself in us; we perceive it by simple self-consciousness. . . . Haiku shows us what we knew all the time but did not know we knew: it shows us that we are poets in so far as we live at all. . . . It takes away as many words as possible between the thing itself and the reader. . . . Nothing is little to him who feels it with great sensibility.'[2]

*T*he following examples were written by a woman in her sixties during a stay of many weeks in the rehabilitation unit. Each is carefully composed of exactly seventeen syllables.

ON WRITING HAIKU

To fold a poem like a paper boat
Sent a-sail to unknown harbours.

MY COTTAGE

Snow drifts, rain beats
Sun bakes, litchen creeps
Moss grows.
Stone walls, slate roof –
Snail's shell.

RADIOTHERAPY

The rising morning moon –
I am a planet,
Bathed in its sterile waves.

PEARL

I will bear this pain
As the oyster its grain of sand
To make a pearl.

BREATH

Air stream –
I try to trap it in my chest cage
Oh! I can't contain it!

These verses encapsulate her experiences and convey them to us with economy, accuracy and poignancy. At the art therapy group they were greatly appreciated and a source of inspiration to the other members.

The box now contains a wide variety of contributions, ranging from sacred verse to funny rhymes. All have a value, one way or another touching the reader and evoking imagery.

13 *Something understood*

Prayer, the Church's banquet, Angels' age,
*   God's breath in man returning to his birth,*
The soul in paraphrase, heart in pilgrimage,
*   The Christian plummet, sounding heaven and earth;*
Engine against the Almighty, sinner's tower,
*   Reversèd thunder, Christ-side-piercing spear,*
The six-days' world transposing in an hour,
*   A kind of tune, which all things hear and fear;*
Softness, and peace, and joy, and love, and bliss,
*   Exalted manna, gladness of the best,*
*   Heaven in ordinary, man well drest,*
The milky way, the bird of Paradise,
*   Church bells beyond the stars heard, the soul's blood,*
*   The land of spices; something understood.*

George Herbert (1593–1633)

It is now possible to consider further the implications and potential for art therapy in cancer care. Since our humanity is shared, regardless of our present and limited roles, let us reconsider this 'understanding' and how it relates to meaning. We find our life through meaning. To approach the end of life with many ordinary sources of meaning stripped away and without having found a direction in which new meaning might lie must be a frightening thought. With the onset of a life-threatening illness a whole scale of values is turned upside down, exposing us to inescapable questions including that of meaning. 'Meaninglessness is a terrible illness. It has to be got over.'[1] 'Meaninglessness inhibits fullness of life and is therefore equivalent to illness. Meaning makes a great many things endurable, perhaps everything.'[2] To conclude this book with such strong statements requires no apology. There is nothing narrow or confining about the word meaning. Given the diversity of material here and of approaches to it, if the point of all search of this nature could be distilled into a single word, 'meaning' would seem to unite this multiplicity of experience.

The questions raised by these experiences are shared by client and therapist alike. No art therapist can enter the arena of life-threatening illness without quickly being brought to realise that these questions are universal, at the same time as they are unique to each person in his or her own circumstances. Since the need to make sense of our lives is in all of us – urgently so for people with major illness – we need to understand a little of what is at stake.

Meaning is never the thing in itself, the seen object – money, for example, has meaning which is different for different people, but the meaning is not the money itself. Meaning can give energy and interest, which can change as meaning changes. Meaning can grow or diminish, become stale and disappear. It is important to find sources of fresh meaning, or to try to recognise

where it might lie. For example, is it possible to trust in the idea that the meaning of the future already exists, and will come without having to be searched for? This would release us to draw meaning from a centredness in the present, within which may lie the hope that someone ill needs so urgently. It does not require much reflection to observe that our orientation towards meaning is changing and varied. However, it is interesting that we respond to a certain scale of meanings – some coarser, some finer – depending on our outer and inner conditions at each moment. A person who is hungry and homeless will have a different orientation from one who is sheltered and fed.

In acknowledging that there are different orders of meaning, we can see that what we seek through the usual modes of self-affirmation in our outer life may predominate for a long time. This need to affirm oneself includes many things – our opinions, the need to succeed, to be right, and so on. Affirmation is also found through talents and pursuits – art, music, writing, scientific knowledge, physical prowess and skills of all sorts. The possible sources of meaning are endless, but lie largely within a scale that is more or less subjective. Our dearly held opinions about, for example, animals or plants may be more subjective than our actual love for them. A search for knowledge of divine things would relate to yet a higher order.

For a person faced with a diagnosis of cancer, regardless of the outcome life may never be the same again. This can be ascribed in part to the aura, or rather stigma, that surrounds the illness. Either immediately or after the initial shock, behind all the fears for the body and anxiety for the future, a process of questioning may appear (or actually reappear, as it is part of our birthright and has been there all the time), formulated as: what am I living for? Who is this person that I call myself? Implicit in these questions and more deeply discerned would be: is there a feeling of myself that is independent of an external influence? Is it possible, through a search to understand, to feel myself beyond all these external factors of diagnosis and illness? 'It is impossible to undertstand life in terms of itself. Taken by itself it is a gigantic muddle. Something must be fitted over life, a system of ideas, to make it have any meaning. Ideas are necessary to transform life into meaning for oneself.'[3] Many people at some stage in their illness sense this muddle; for some, clarity later seems to reappear. Although this is an inner condition for which words may not find a place, art therapy can nurture and accelerate the clarifying process which is difficult to evaluate in words, let alone by scientific measurement.

What role does the art therapist play, and what does she have to offer? In the words of T. S. Eliot: 'A condition of complete simplicity / (Costing not less than everything).'[4] What is this 'simplicity', what is this 'everything'? I have considered and reconsidered this phrase over the ten years that I have been engaged in this work; a wish to find such a 'condition of complete simplicity' has attracted me over and over again when faced with a patient with cancer. Whether it is at the time of diagnosis, recurrence, or in the later stages when hope has to change its focus, I have often felt that the person was requiring something of me that would not be served by words, especially when I recognise that words can just be a noise behind which I can protect myself from an awareness of my own mortality as well as theirs. Often in unprepared moments, a therapist may have recourse to words and sentiments at best stereotyped or at worst meaningless or even dismissive, merely to retain her own sense of equilibrium and competence in her role. Words, ostensibly communicative, can also be used defensively, to shield oneself from the distress of another. And in the late stages of cancer, even medicine is mute.

A social worker once told me about a furious patient who had apparently been told that she could not be offered any further treatment in the way of chemotherapy, radiotherapy and so on, but that she might like to try art therapy! Put like this, it must have seemed to the patient like a final acknowledgement of failure by her doctors. What strategies or forces can come to our aid when this position is reached? 'A condition of complete simplicity.' Both therapist and patient should consider the meaning of this phrase. Reflecting upon the word 'simplicity', the word 'attention' comes into mind. They seem in a way to complement each other, as though both are needed to achieve the 'completeness' spoken of. This word, 'attention', now gives new meaning to the second phrase: 'Costing not less that everything.' Patients engaging in art therapy can often be observed as utterly involved with their work. This commitment of attention to what they are doing, even if brief, brings relief and complete respite from powerful inner anxiety – which until the moment when the creative process took over might have been enslaving their attention, indeed their whole being.

'Attention', 'everything' – perhaps the words are even synonymous. We all need attention, but how difficult it is to give it to oneself in a real sense. A hospitalised person with a number and a case history needs the attention of others even more, as affirmation that they exist as well as their illness. What is the cost, what has to be given up for a 'condition of complete simplicity', or 'attention'? For the therapist, in order to prepare to be with others needing her attention, there are several things – the mind, endlessly occupied with dreams, plans, associations; the emotions, with their underlying climate of feeling, shifting and unpredictable, and the physical body with its demands to be satisfied, along with its tensions and compulsion to fidget. How does one relinquish all this for a condition of complete attention? Even stillness is difficult. Again, Eliot recognises this: 'Teach us to care and not to care / Teach us to sit still.'[5]

This whole question is of great importance for art therapists working in cancer care. Unlike art therapy in psychiatry, in cancer it is not a remedial process. Psychopathology may exist in a person from the past, but generally it is the psychological effects of being diagnosed and living with cancer and its treatment that are the main issue. The aims of art therapy in this context are not to establish autonomy, improve relationships or uncover root causes of problems; rather, they are to facilitate important processes that, on differing levels, can substantially help someone to cope with illness and uncertainty. The art therapist provides a means through image-making for the patient to undertake his own journey towards a deeper understanding of himself and his situation, and supports and acknowledges whatever it may bring him. The need for attentive listening, therefore, is crucial, as it is for any health professional. To be really listened to is quite unusual in day-to-day life, and something of a luxury. It can be quite a shock: 'For most of us there is only the unattended / Moment.'[6] However silent the listening, if it is genuinely attentive it transmits far more energy than many wise words delivered without the substance of that attention behind them.

'A condition of complete simplicity': for two people to communicate fully it would seem this condition must be present. An individual can be suddenly brought to this point through shock. Illness and suffering over a period of time can also pare a human being down to a much simpler, less complicated state. The art therapist needs to recognise the much simpler condition at which people arrive when they have had cancer for some time. She may sense that the patients with whom she comes into contact are in a very different state from herself.

Can the issues raised here for patient and therapist be addressed together? Are there unifying elements between the two apparently differing viewpoints? If we were considering art therapy in other settings – for example, psychiatry, education and social services – the conclusion might be more clear-cut. In oncology different and profound issues are involved and the boundaries are less simple. Since death is a mystery, it is not surprising that the powerful, intimate, even primeval process that can be set in train by art therapy evokes incomprehension in those who look only to science to provide all the answers to human affliction. But for those who find themselves subject to an illness such as cancer and for those who are drawn to share their questions, new possibilities may be approached through art in therapy. While both patient and therapist may find much to appreciate through the use of materials and exploration of images, they both need to find ways of accepting that questions concerning life, illness and death can only be entertained, not answered. However, through the creative process they may be led to ask such questions more deeply. Intimations may be offered that serve to increase the sense of wonder at the magnitude of the mystery. Fear may diminish, and awe take its place.

The art therapist, inevitably, will find herself entering uncharted psychological country. Talking with the patient and viewing his images, she may find that a deep level in her is touched by the emergence of his 'soul' work. 'From the soul's viewpoint, there is little difference between patient and therapist. Both words in their roots refer to an attentive devotion, waiting on and waiting for.'[7] Together, patient and therapist respond sensitively to the resonance of the picture between them, exploring it with great delicacy. This may be a rare and unexpected event for the patient, the value of which is impossible to define. For the therapist to remain with him, actively attending, is work indeed.

If a patient dies, the therapist is inevitably left to contemplate the memory of the person and all the events that occurred. It is then her task, when she finds herself with another patient at a similar stage, to try to sustain her sense of wonder and to accept more deeply that there is no end or limitation to this enigma. The therapist may experience a sense of loss, but also a cognition that what was shared was both within and also beyond our ordinary sense of time. Through the tangible evidence of the art work, it remains a living encounter whenever it is recalled. The art work may retain its life for years, conferring a kind of immortality on the patient.

Gradually, the therapist receives and carries within herself (as well as on paper) more and more testimonies to the link between human beings and things that are beyond description. Hope is always present – not just for the future as we understand it, but for expansion in other dimensions of experience which some call 'eternity'. Such a hope is nearly always to be found in the art work – both the therapist and the patient's loved ones can take comfort in the fact that the dying person saw more than they did, and that there is much beyond the evidence of the senses.

I truly hope that in the telling of these individual stories something complete has emerged, to show that there are many sides to a life-threatening illness. If the opportunity for a creative response is presented, there is no knowing what heights can be scaled or depths plumbed in one individual's journey.

Art therapy: the professional context

Joan Woddis

Vice-President, British Association of Art Therapists

There seems at present to be a growing awareness of the importance of inner feelings and the inheritance of individual history – ideas that, until relatively recently, were largely confined to psychoanalytic thought. It is a striking paradox that this apparent need to understand our lives more fully coexists among many of us in our culture with feelings of powerlessness and frustration. It is against this backdrop that the concepts of psychoanalysis have gained prominence within popular culture and produced the climate in which the practice of art therapy as a discrete profession has developed.

The practice of art therapy in the UK dates back to the late 1940s, when artists began to be employed in psychiatric hospitals. These practitioners sought to work therapeutically with their patients in studio settings; they were supported by certain psychiatrists and psychoanalysts who had found patients' paintings to be an invaluable element in the curative process. Many of their colleagues offered their psychological skills and understanding to the first art therapists.

The principle was established in those early years that art therapists are primarily artists. It is important that those who wish to examine our profession realise that this basic understanding continues today. It is demonstrated in the context of training and in the parameters both of our career structure and our professional organisation. The establishment in 1964 of the British Association of Art Therapists brought together a small group of dedicated practitioners, working largely in psychiatric hospitals. They recognised that their transactions with their patients were something other than technical instruction, other than the interpretation of images and other than counselling or advice-giving. It was something else, something unique. They saw themselves as offering an essentially 'alternative' form of treatment and thus they were outsiders in a scientific environment.

Steadily they began to develop and modify their practice, to affirm that providing the means for patients to paint is not always enough. They realised that art therapy is a psychodynamic process, based upon a relationship between patient and therapist (the 'therapeutic alliance'), and that the elements of transference, projection and fantasy are manifested in imagery as well as in discourse and behaviour. They sought to integrate these in a triangular relationship of therapist, client and image, and began to draw on the theories of psychoanalysis and developmental psychology. The profession began to grow.

In 1982, the then Department of Health and Social Security recognised the profession and established a structure for its clinical practice. This brought into existence a defined salary scale, the validation of training procedures, and the official acceptance of art therapists as part of treatment teams. The British Association of Art Therapists, which at the time had around 180 members, set about developing other strengths of professional organisation. Its aim was to establish a career structure and recognition for art therapists in whatever settings they might work.

A professional register was set up in 1984, listing British art therapists (and others who had completed a British training) for use by Health and Social Service managers and the general public. Today there are just on 1,000 registered members.

Following a detailed survey of the working conditions of art therapists, a code of professional practice was devised in 1982 which attempted to lay down principles of sound practice. In the mid 1990s this was modified and improved, and it now forms our code of ethics.

Training courses had developed in the mid 1970s; from their inception, the central principle was defined and held intrinsic to training that art therapists should come from an art background, either from a fine art training or as specialist art teachers. Consequently, training programmes have to be at postgraduate level. There are five such courses operating in British universities today.

Over the years, the institutional context of art therapy has broadened. Although a career structure has yet to be established in the social and community services, the profession is recognised and its practice widespread. The art therapist's role in child psychiatry, family therapy and special education is generally accepted. British art therapists have found themselves working with many confirmed or suspected cases of child abuse, where imagery plays a vital role in making manifest the history, memories and wishes of the client. Art therapists may be found practising in drug rehabilitation and in custodial care with young offenders, or within psychiatric units in adult prisons. In early 1997, British art, music and drama therapy became registered as professions supplementary to medicine by Act of Parliament; its practitioners were invited to take up state registration. The profession had come of age, but further changes were already afoot.

Art therapists have had to re-examine their practice in the light of new situations, client groups, staff teams and management structures. Over the years, their techniques and processes had evolved largely for the treatment of patients in closed psychiatric institutions. It was acknowledged that art therapy could no longer remain a homogenised service with the same experience offered to all patients, but rather that a flexible approach should be taken, a constellation of different treatments: it was clear that art therapy might be useful to a very wide range of patients. A belief (in some respects a mythology) that the art-making process has an intrinsic healing quality continues to come under fierce scrutiny. The idea that the act of artistic creation is of itself healing suggests that the effect does not necessarily involve the intervention or even the presence of another person. British art therapists, however, remain convinced that the healing process is built on the therapeutic relationship, however fleeting that may be.

Art therapists moved comparatively recently into the field of palliative care. It requires practice of great subtlety, compassion and humility to work – often in very brief moments – with those facing life-threatening illness and death itself. Art therapy has begun to be available to patients in hospices, AIDS and HIV treatment units, and to those suffering from cancer. Camilla Connell has established herself as a leading practitioner in this field, developing an approach of great sensitivity which is uniquely her own. This book stands as a fascinating and moving testament to her patients, and is a worthy addition to the literature of her profession.

Art therapy, psychological support and cancer care

Ian B. Kerr, MD, MRCPsych.

Department of Psychological Medicine, Royal Marsden NHS Trust, London

It is a considerable pleasure to have been asked to make a contribution to Camilla Connell's extremely moving and illuminating book. As a psychiatrist and psychotherapist working with many of the same patients, I am very aware of how valuable art therapy (and other creative therapies) can be in enabling patients with serious, often life-threatening and fatal illnesses to make sense of and cope with their experience, both in an immediate as well as a more general sense. Her book prompts many reflections on my part about the importance of creativity in therapy, how it overlaps with the sort of psychological support we in our department are also asked to provide, about the place of both in our health service and, finally, the significance of all this in our present-day, 'post-modern', Western culture.

It is very clear from the vivid and empathetic descriptions of work in the book and, above all, from the testimonies of the patients themselves, both pictorial and verbal, how powerful, necessary and often surprising such experiences can be. I have certainly often referred patients for art therapy who were finding it hard to deal with the often disturbing and powerful emotions provoked by the onset of illness; I have found that it enables exploration of feelings as well as communication and personal fulfilment to occur in a way that I could not otherwise imagine happening. This is, I think, due in large part to the way in which such work gets past the normal inhibitions and defences that are associated with expressing oneself, whether verbally or by attempts at formal art work. Importantly, it also clearly permits the expression of emotions such as anger, sadness and fear, which may be difficult to do otherwise – particularly if the patient feels afflicted by the fashion for 'positive thinking' which can in itself be a terrible burden. Art therapy may also facilitate our approach as psychologists, as well as that of the other staff directly involved in cancer treatment. It seems to me that this book and its contents illustrate, in a remarkable and unique way, just how 'archetypally' powerful are the emotions and thoughts, often only partly conscious, that are stirred up in this situation and that need to be addressed and made sense of. These feelings are also evident in the vivid and often disturbing dreams which such patients frequently report.

This work also appears to perform several very important functions, apart from the obvious 'representational' one evidenced by the images themselves. At another level, as with many other therapies, the art therapist is discharging an important role not only as facilitator but also as 'witness' to the struggle and often the anguish of the patient in facing and making sense of destructive and intrusive illness. It is clearly of critical importance that through the therapist a secure setting exists without which such work cannot occur. The psychoanalyst D. W. Winnicott notably discussed how creative achievement depends on the existence of just such a psychologically secure place (his 'third area', deriving from early mother–infant experiences), where the trust and 'playfulness' necessary to allow creative responses to flourish exists.[1] I am also struck by the fact that something concrete and visible is produced that seems highly significant and that may have magical or 'talismanic' quality[2] – traditionally, a talisman was something worn to ward off evil spirits or that had special healing properties. I am struck, too, by similarities between these special 'jointly produced' objects and the practice of the increasingly popular cognitive-analytic therapy (CAT), in which the production of an explicit, written, joint 'reformulation' of a patient's story and problematic issues is central to the therapy.[3] CAT is also used in our department, and such reformulation also represents a witnessing as well as an interpreting and recording of an individual's story. The linked themes of 'narrative' and 'witnessing' have become much discussed as important functions that occur implicitly in most verbal psychotherapies, in contrast to the traditional stress laid on the interpretative role of the therapist.

The question of whether one's story is 'heard', whether it matters and implicitly whether one belongs and whether one's life has any significance seems a critical one which presents itself particularly poignantly in our highly individualised, fragmented 'post-modern' society. This essentially religious enquiry was regarded by Jung as central to the human condition, yet the support, consolation or certainty of formal religion is increasingly absent among patients, even those with professed beliefs, as is any sustaining ritual. These issues are particularly important in the context of the culture in which we now live.[4] It seems to me that coping with and adjusting to illness has become increasingly difficult in our fragmented and individualised society, in which there is an increasing expectation, verging on a delusory sense of 'entitlement', that we should all live long and healthy lives over which we have complete control. When illness does occur, the consequence is a sense of outrage and injustice – especially so, of course, in the genuinely tragic instances when illness occurs prematurely as in a child or the parent of young children. This is in marked contrast to the situation in developing countries where illness is common and life is still 'cheap', and where Western expectations – fuelled by modern science and medicine, as well as our individualistic culture – do not exist. In reality, it is remarkable that in our culture people can now live to quite an advanced age without directly encountering death among family or friends – impossible even a couple of generations ago. The transition from considering death as an 'if' question to a 'when and how' question may therefore come very late in life, excluding death from serious contemplation and contributing to these delusory, collective expectations.

The individual or nuclear family that does encounter serious illness may suddenly find that interest, empathy and support may not be forthcoming from members of the community at large – who, in their own individualistic quest for achievement and fulfilment, do not and possibly cannot interest themselves in those with illness. This ostracism and stigmatism has been perhaps most evident in the case of victims of the AIDS epidemic, which has afflicted us in the last decade or so. The same demoralising sense of isolation is, in my experience, very common among sufferers from cancer, and also among those who have survived it. The latter, often left with a permanent sense of insecurity, frequently find it very hard to reintegrate into our 'collectively deluded' culture, much in the way that traumatised war veterans do.

All of this occurs in a culture with little sense of common purpose and in which, in the phrase of the post-modern philosopher, any sense of a 'grand narrative' is dead. It is a state of affairs that reminds me of a reportedly traditional Cossack saying, that 'even death is good if you belong to the tribe'. In the West it is also extremely difficult and alien for us to try to adopt the position of many oriental philosophies, of 'detachment' from worldly aspirations leading to a calm acceptance of illness or mortality. Aversion to and ignorance of death in our present culture is, after all, aversion to and ignorance of what is our natural and inevitable end. Many analysts suggest that an essential part of the process of individuation consists in confronting our mortality and being able to come to terms with it.[5] Failure to do so must clearly have an enormous effect on how we lead our lives, since it must have the inevitable consequence of anger and disbelief – the reaction I frequently encounter of 'why me?' I vividly remember one particularly angry patient who had been a wealthy and successful businessman; on reflection, he finally agreed that he had probably thought he was 'immortal'.

There seem to be considerable similarities and much overlap between the work of our department and that of the art therapist, although obviously psychologists use different 'treatment' approaches and at times our work must employ pharmacological or more formal psychological approaches to enable patients to function. Ultimately, however, we are all addressing the same issue: the search for meaning and purpose in life in the face of an unexpected and potentially overwhelming threat to it which can easily pitch an individual into a state of extreme and disabling 'ontological anxiety' (in the phrase of the theologian Paul Tillich).

Although creativity in the obvious sense is central

to the work of art therapy, a broader notion of creativity is also fundamental to the work of most psychotherapies, albeit through verbal rather than pictorial means. This is creativity as the exploration of meaning and its symbolic communication as a central feature of our existence, as discussed, for example, by Marion Milner and Charles Rycroft.[6] Milner writes of 'the creative roots of our existence'. This process of symbolisation – the synthesising of previously unknown thoughts and feelings, conscious or unconscious, into something of irreducible, communicative complexity – is described as the 'transcendent' function in the Jungian tradition, which historically has placed great emphasis on this aspect of psychotherapy.[7] However, contemporary writers, such as the American psychoanalyst Thomas Ogden, also appear to have moved away from the historically rather reductive attitude towards art and creativity by placing intersubjectivity, as mediated by symbolic activity, central to the therapeutic enterprise. Thus he states: 'symbols help create us as subjects. To deny a patient the transformative potential of symbols is to deny him the means by which he might attempt to achieve psychological change.'[8]

The relation of creativity to illness, death and dying has been notably explored by Rosemary Gordon in her classic text on dying and creating.[9] Based on a wide-ranging study of anthropological literature and psychotherapeutic (notably Jungian) theory, as well as her own analytic experience, it suggests that historically man's whole life has been preoccupied by death and dying and by theories or 'myths' to account for it. She also suggests that addressing and accounting for death is a necessary part of growth and individuation – in its absence, it is hard to live or die well. She explores fascinating parallels between the process of creativity – and its requirement that one is open to fusion-like (arguably womb- or early infant-like) experiences and an associated abandonment of 'ego'-dominated modes of thinking – and that of dying. Such experiences, notably described by mystics and artists as well as scientists, have been variously described as 'participation mystique' by Jung and as 'oceanic feeling' by Freud. Whether, in conjunction with the well-documented capacity of our species for violence, these states constitute evidence for the existence of a 'death instinct' (as postulated by many analytic writers) seems to me altogether more contentious. What the nature of these processes highlights, however, is that a certain ontological security is required to enter them, as arguably is also the case in order to contemplate death and dying. This would be both difficult and frightening to achieve in a state of anxiety due to the absence of a sense of meaning and belonging – whether caused by damaging early childhood attachment experiences or later social experience. Paradoxically, being able to achieve a state of mature 'detachment' appears to require the earlier existence of psychological security and 'attachment'.

These issues are surely at the heart of working therapeutically (whether with words or pictures) with patients facing fatal illnesses such as cancer; they are the reason why what therapies have to offer is so important – art therapy, in particular, with its explicit production of meaningful symbolic objects. Thus it seems that as long as one is involved creatively in trying to make sense of things and communicate, one is not only living but living well, and challenging the despair and hopelessness that can otherwise easily feel overwhelming. I am reminded of the assertion reportedly made by a musician inmate of the concentration camp at Terezin: 'as long as I can create, death does not exist . . .' Similarly, a patient of mine who had been a talented designer and who continued drawing until shortly before his death, replied when asked about his creative activities, 'Creativity? . . . creativity is everything . . .'

The focus on the importance of symbol- or sign-mediated behaviour in human culture has obvious common ground with the approach, stemming from the work of Bakhtin, described nowadays as 'dialogism'.[10] This sees human cultural and symbolically mediated behaviour as well as the existence of the self (largely understood as a social 'construct' and as a 'narrative'), as occurring in the context of pre-existing cultural dialogue (or 'voices'). These, internalised, actually constitute and determine much of our consciousness and sense of self; in turn, they contribute to the continuation of our culture. Such 'voices' can be identified and worked with in psychotherapy,[11] and of course constitute much of the material on which psychoanalysts have historically focused in 'transference'. What seems particularly interesting is the idea that our individual existences and our culture can be conceived of within the theoretical framework of 'dialogism'. This could suggest the existence of some more long-lasting social nexus in which we participate, in a sense perpetually or 'immortally'. A statement by Bakhtin comes close to suggesting this:

The contexts of dialogue are without limit. They extend into the deepest part and the most distant future. Even meanings born in dialogues of the remotest past will never be finally grasped once and for all, for they will always be renewed in later dialogue. At any present moment there are great masses of forgotten meanings, but these will be recalled again at a given moment in the dialogue's later course when it will be given new life. For nothing is absolutely dead: every meaning will someday have its home-coming festival . . .[12]

This passage has obvious resonances, perhaps not accidental, with the famous deathbed speech in Boris Pasternak's *Doctor Zhivago* which is often used in humanist funeral ceremonies. It concludes:

> *However far back you go in your memory, it is always some external, active manifestation of yourself that you come across in your identity, in the work of your hands, in your family, in other people, this is what you are . . . And what now? You have always been in others and you will remain in others. And what does it matter to you if later on it is called your memory? This will be part of you, the real you that enters the future and becomes a part of it.*

I have certainly found that discussions of such subjects can be very helpful and reassuring in a quasi-religious way both to patients and myself, gripped as we are by ontological anxiety and anguish in the face of illness and the prospect of death. The images of art therapy clearly appear to be participants in such 'dialogue'.

This perspective seems also to bear striking parallels, or indeed to share common ground, with the similar idea implicit in modern genetics. Given that all living organisms on earth (from water lilies to Einstein or Mozart) are made up of the same 'building blocks' of DNA, and that we are all nothing more than random assortments of these same genes, we are therefore in a sense all 'immortal' as long as life remains on earth, since these genes will all remain, both in our immediate relatives but also in all other organisms. Curiously, these notions seem to overlap with some oriental ideas of the permanence of our lives; I have found that they can help in discussion of the task of readjusting and detaching, which constitutes part of the work of dying.

It is very clear to me that the work and activity described in Camilla Connell's book play important roles within the overall context of a cancer hospital as well as, arguably, of the culture beyond it. The work she does, as well as my own to some extent, enables patients to function and cope in practical ways with their illness and treatment; to that extent it actually facilitates and permits the work of treating the tumour to go on. Certainly there is evidence that psychological wellbeing contributes both to the ability to cope as well as, in some cases, to actual relapse-free survival. I know it also relieves the burden on other staff most involved in supporting and caring for patients who may be very distressed and disabled. Often such staff, notably nurses, are well motivated to attempt to work with these issues, but simply do not have the time or perhaps the formal training and support to do so. In addition, they face the demands of a busy hospital routine in which, even today, there still lingers a somewhat disciplinarian attitude towards the exploration and communication of the feelings of patients and staff (including doctors) in coping with these stressful and emotionally demanding illnesses. The implication is that these feelings should somehow be coped with and repressed or, at best, referred on to be dealt with by professionals such as ourselves, with our own very limited resources. This remains the case despite the literature for addressing and working with such feelings both to improve quality of care and to prevent staff 'burn-out'.

An interesting extension of art therapy work would lie in offering it to members of staff. Reactions to the value of our therapeutic work vary considerably around our hospital, from chief executive through to the various professionals and ancillary staff, whether it is conceived of as a central task or an occasional individual problem. Most, I think, would value the work at least on an occasional basis, but tend to regard it as a rather 'fringe' or luxury component of care. If we take seriously the stated aims of our rehabilitation service to address and treat all aspects of care, including the psychosocial and spiritual, then the work described in this book ought to be placed centrally and resourced and respected accordingly. I note rather sadly, however, that the latest business plan summary of our hospital trust makes no direct mention of such services or their importance, beyond a rhetorical commitment towards a 'patient-focused approach'.

Although the value of art therapy is very clear from the examples presented in this book, it will be important in the future for the creative therapies in general to present formal, evidence-based justification for their provision. It is difficult to measure the outcomes of these therapies, a fact that those who minimise their importance must bear in mind. It will be important to establish, for example, whether patients with particular symptoms or probems are helped by art therapy in particular, as opposed to other approaches. Already such trials of art therapy are under way for psychiatric patients, and I would be confident that, even using the crude outcome measures currently available, there will be a clear demonstration of its efficacy in cancer care. Whether this is then translated into the purchase and provision of such services will depend on the attitudes of purchasers to the values and issues discussed above as well as, critically, the demand from patients and relatives for such resources to be routinely available as part of their care. Given the recognised lack of funds for our health service, taxpayers will have to think seriously about their priorities and whether these services are worth hard cash in our culture.

One of the merits of this book is that it implicitly raises such issues for critical examination in general – in our culture at large, as well as more practically in cancer treatment. If it also reminds us all of the centrality and inevitability of death and illness in our existence and the importance of our common quest for meaning, it will not only make it easier for cancer sufferers to live and cope with their illness but will also diminish the stigma and isolation that compounds their difficulty in doing so. In acknowledging the very great effort and commitment put in by Camilla Connell over the years, we ought seriously to consider that we really need one of her (at least!) in every unit in the hospital. I very much hope that this important book receives the attention it deserves, so that it may contribute fully to an appreciation and discussion of the central importance of attending to the meaning of our individual experience – both in cancer care and, more generally, in our fragmented culture wherever it ultimately evolves.

*N*otes

FOREWORD (pp. 10 – 11)

1. C. G. Jung, Psychological Types, Routledge Kegan Paul, London, 1923, p. 311.

CHAPTER 2 (pp. 22 – 25)

1. C. G. Jung, commentary on *The Secret of the Golden Flower*, trans. Richard Wilhelm, Kegan Paul, London, 1942.

CHAPTER 6 (pp. 52 – 61)

1. From D. H. Lawrence, *Complete Poems*, Heinemann, London, 1964.

2. Myriam Senez, unpublished essay written during art therapy training, 1998.

3. Plotinus, *The Enneads*, trans. Stephen McKenna, Faber and Faber, London, 1969, p. 63.

CHAPTER 8 (pp. 76 – 89)

1. Simone Weil, 'The Love of God and Affliction', in *On Science, Necessity and the Love of God*, essays collected, trans. and ed. by Richard Rees, Oxford University Press, Oxford, 1968, p. 182.

2. Dylan Thomas, *Collected Poems 1934–1952*, J. M. Dent and Sons, London, 1952, p. 116.

3. Acts of John, Apocryphal New Testament, King James translation, Oxford University Press, London, 1924, 'fragment' 96, p. 254.

4. Simone Weil, op. cit., p. 181.

CHAPTER 9 (pp. 90 – 97)

1. C. G. Jung, *Collected Works*, vol. V, *Symbols of Transformation*, Routledge Kegan Paul, London, 1956, p. 288.

CHAPTER 10 (pp. 98 – 107)

1. Roger Cook, *The Tree of Life*, Thames and Hudson, London, 1974, p. 27.

2. Johannus Lydus, 'Di Mensibus: IV', quoted in Louis Charbonneau Lassau, *The Bestiary of Christ*, Parabola, New York, 1991, p. 211.

3. Lanoe-Villene, 'Le Livre de symboles', quoted in ibid., p. 212.

4. Quoted in George Lechler, 'The Tree of Life in Indo-European and Islamic Culture', *Ars Islamica*, vol. VI, 1937.

CHAPTER 11 (pp. 108 – 117)

1. S. Klossowski de Rola, *Alchemy*, Thames and Hudson, London, 1973, p. 7.

2. C. G. Jung, *Collected Works*, vol. V, *Symbols of Transformation*, p. 231.

3. Ibid., vol. V, p. 222.

4. From ibid., vol. XII, *Psychology and Alchemy*, p. 399.

5. Ibid., vol. V, p. 222.

6. Cook, op. cit.

7. 'Brhadaranyaka Upanishad', v. 10, quoted in Coomeraswamy, *Selected Papers on Traditional Art and Symbolism*, ed. Roger Lipsey, Princeton University Press, 1977.

8. Coomeraswamy, op. cit., p. 406, referring to Rumi, 'The Mathnawi', IV 3164, VI 1622 and Meister Eckhart, 'The Sea'.

9. Ibid., p. 409.

10. Quoted in C. G. Jung, *Collected Works*, vol. XII, p. 305.

CHAPTER 12 (pp. 118 – 125)

1. *The New Oxford Book of English Verse*, chosen and edited by Helen Gardner, Clarendon Press, Oxford, 1972.

2. Quoted in R. H. Blyth, Preface to vol. I, *Haiku*, 4 vols., Hokuseido, Japan, 1949.

CHAPTER 13 (pp. 126 – 131)

1. Maurice Nicoll, *The Mark*, Watkins, London, 1954, p. 19.

2. C. G. Jung, *Memories, Dreams, Reflections*, Collins and Routledge Kegan Paul, London, 1963, p. 313.

3. Nicoll, op. cit., p. 88.

4. T. S. Eliot, 'Four Quartets: Little Gidding', *Collected Poems*, Faber and Faber, London, 1969.

5. T. S. Eliot, 'Ash Wednesday', ibid.

6. T. S. Eliot, 'Four Quartets: The Dry Salvages', ibid.

7. J. Hillman, *The Dream and the Underworld*, Harper and Row, New York, 1979, p. 65.

PSYCHOLOGICAL SUPPORT AND CANCER CARE (pp. 132 – 143)

1. D. W. Winnicott, *Playing and Reality*, Tavistock, London, 1971.

2. As described by the analytical art therapist Joy Schaverein in *The Revealing Image: Analytical Art Therapy in Theory and Practice*, Routledge, London, 1992.

3. A. Ryle, ed., *Cognitive-analytic Therapy: Developments in Theory and Practice*, Wiley, Chichester, 1995.

4. Attitudes to death and dying, widely differing in various cultures, have been thought-provokingly discussed in C. Murray-Parkes, P. Laungani and B. Young, eds., *Death and Bereavement across Cultures*, Routledge, London, 1996.

5. See, for example, Rosemary Gordon, *Dying and Creating: A Search for Meaning*, The Society of Analytical Psychology, London, 1978.

6. Marion Milner, 'Psycho-analysis and Art', in *Psycho-analysis and Contemporary Thought*, ed. J. D. Sutherland, Hogarth Press, London, 1958; Charles Rycroft, *Imagination and Reality*, Hogarth, London, 1968.

7. See note 5.

8. T. H. Ogden, *Subjects of Analysis*, Jason Aronson, Northvale, N.J., 1994.

9. See note 5.

10. See M. Holquist, *Dialogism: Bakhtin and his World*, Routledge, London, 1990. The further implications of this work for psychotherapy have been recently explored by Mikael Leiman, in 'Procedures as dialogical sequences: A revised version of the fundamental concept in cognitive-analytic therapy', *British Journal of Medical Psychology*, vol. 70, 1997, pp. 193–207.

11. See ibid., Leiman.

12. See Holquist, op. cit.

*F*urther reading

Amanda Pratt and Michele Wood, eds., *Art Therapy in Palliative Care – The Creative Response*, Routledge, London, 1998

Martina Thomson, *On Art and Therapy. An Exploration*, Free Association Books, London, 1997

Caroline Case and Tessa Dalley, *The Handbook of Art Therapy*, Routledge, London, 1992

Patrice Guex, *An Introduction to Psycho-Oncology*, trans. Heather Goodare, Routledge, London, 1994

Michael Kearney, *Mortally Wounded: Stories of Soul Pain, Death and Healing*, Marino Books, Dublin, 1996

Without the material support of the following organisations, it would not have been possible to publish this book. For their generosity and trust in the eventual outcome I am extremely grateful.

The Omega Foundation was founded in 1987 by Dr Susan Bach, who worked mainly in Zurich on ways in which spontaneous painting could help physicians to understand the psychological and physical causes of serious illness in children. It provides funding for projects that the Trustees feel will achieve any of the following:
– to assist research into new methods of alleviating the suffering of emotionally disturbed or seriously ill patients;
– to help enhance the skills of physicians and other health professionals to assist patients suffering from severe illness, including suicidal tendencies, to discover their own inner resources and come to terms with their illness;
– to help support specialised training of health professionals into ways of assisting severely ill patients and their families;
– to help disseminate the results of such research by means of group discussion or conferences.

For further details and applications, enquiries should be sent to:
Dr Christopher Donovan
25 Middleway, London NW11 6SH.

The Corinne Burton Memorial Trust was set up to commemorate Corinne Burton, an artist and mother who died from cancer at an early age. She spoke of how she derived great benefit from art during her illness.

The Trust aims to increase the provision of art therapy for cancer sufferers by funding training and work placements for art therapists working with cancer patients. It has endowed Goldsmith's College, University of London, with a bursary to pay the fees for one student each year; once they are qualified, the Trust continues to fund them in their workplaces at a hospice or oncology unit. The Trust is also funding Corinne Burton Art Therapists at the Royal London and the Royal Marsden Hospitals, and at the Edenhall Marie Curie Centre in Hampstead, north London.

As its work expands nationwide, the Trust, a registered charity, is always grateful for any support. Donations may be sent to:
The Corinne Burton Memorial Trust
c/o Citroen Wells, Devonshire House
1 Devonshire Street, London WIN 2DR.

Zeneca Pharmaceuticals
I am extremely grateful to the Grants Committee of Zeneca Pharmaceuticals for considering it appropriate to support this project.

Camilla Connell
London 1998

Useful addresses

British Association of Art Therapists
5 Tavistock Place
London WC1H 9SN

The Creative Response
Art Therapy in Palliative Care, Aids, Cancer & Loss
The Old Coal House
Station Road
Ardleigh
Colchester CO7 7RR

The Creative Response is an organisation of registered art therapists working in palliative care, AIDS, cancer and loss. The group was formed to provide support for all art therapists working in this field, and to promote awareness of its relevance to allied professions and the general public. The register is constantly being updated.

Accredited training programmes are available at the following establishments:

Art Psychotherapy Unit
Goldsmith's College
University of London
23 St James
New Cross
London SE14 6NW

School of Art and Design
University of Hertfordshire
Manor Road
Hatfield
Hertfordshire AL10 9TL

City of Bath College
Department of Visual Arts
Avon Street
Bath BA1 1UP

School of Art Therapy
Queen Margaret College
Leith Campus
Duke Street
Edinburgh EH6 8HF

Centre for Psychotherapeutic Studies
University of Sheffield
16 Claremont Crescent
Sheffield S10 2TA